75 YEARS OF
FORMULA ONE

First published in the UK by Sona Books, an imprint of Danann Media Publishing Limited

Original material for the Legendary Drivers reproduced by courtesy of Future Publishing 2022

CAT NO. SON0657

Book design: Kevin Gardner
Editor: Martin Corteel
Proof reader: Cameron Thurlow
Cover design: Darren Grice

Contributors:
Rob Clark, Natalie Denton, Jamie Frier, Charles Ginger, Steve Jenkins, Scott Reeves, David Smith, Iain Spragg and Bruce Vigar

Printed in E.U.

ISBN: 978-1-917259-24-8

75 YEARS OF FORMULA ONE

sona BOOKS

No through road. Nigel Mansell, in his clearly faster Williams, desperately tries to overtake master operator Ayrton Senna at the Monaco Grand Prix in 1992

CONTENTS

The pinnacle of motorsport with a global TV audience far in excess of half a billion each and every year, Formula One is a sporting phenomenon that unfailingly entertains. Born back in 1950 at the British Grand Prix, staged at the iconic Silverstone Circuit, the sport proudly celebrates its 75th birthday in 2025 and remains synonymous with breakneck thrills and spills, engineering innovation and, above all, unforgettable personalities

INTRODUCTION

Over the years the cars propelled at improbable speeds all over the world have changed almost beyond recognition but, at its heart, F1 is still the same and beguilingly simple battle between an intrepid, select few to lap the fastest at any cost. Courage, talent, mechanical excellence, as well as the frequent vagaries of the weather, all combine to make any given Grand Prix weekend unmissable.

Legendary Argentinean Juan Manuel Fangio was F1's first superstar, winning the newly founded Driver's Championship five times in the embryonic 1950s, and since his golden era the competition has given sport some of its most famous names from Ayrton Senna to Michael Schumacher and Alain Prost to Lewis Hamilton. Record-breaking reigning world champion Max Verstappen is the latest fearless driver to have scaled the summit of F1 and, in claiming four consecutive crowns, transcend motorsport.

As it has done since its inception, F1 racing attracts some of the automotive industry's leading lights in pursuit of a coveted Constructor's Championship title. In the early days, it was iconic names such as Lotus, Cooper and Alfa Romeo spearheading the Grand Prix charge while, more recently, historic yet thoroughly modern car behemoths Mercedes and Ferrari have tested their mettle on the annual F1 circuit. The margins between success and failure remain miniscule but each year the teams return with dreams of speed and silverware.

Celebrating the fascinating and always dramatic history of the sport and its milestone anniversary, chronicling its most memorable races, greatest drivers and controversies, *75 Years of Formula One* is the glorious, definitive story of the lives lived – and sometimes tragically lost – at full throttle.

Juan Manuel Fangio on his way to winning the 1951 French Grand Prix in an Alfa Romeo

Pioneered by German engineering excellence and a French passion for speed, motor racing took its first, tentative steps in the 1890s, but it was the dawn of the 20th century that witnessed the sport, despite being haunted by frequent tragedy and controversy, explode into life

THE ORIGINS OF FORMULA ONE

Paul Baras in his Brasier at the Circuit des Ardennes in 1906

HOW IT ALL BEGAN

They invented the wheel, so why the ancient Mesopotamians weren't hurtling around racetracks 3,500 years ago is beyond the understanding of anyone who loves motor racing. The world had to wait for the Mycenaean Greeks to turn up, it seems, (thankfully they did) before spectators could enjoy the thrill of wheeled speed racing; pottery fragments appear to confirm that these fearless pioneers were charging around in chariots sometime around 1600–1100 BC. What on earth did the ancients do with their Sunday afternoons before that?

And another thing; why did it then take until 1886 to produce the first motorcar?

Fine, we won't go into that, but thank you Herr Karl Benz for his Benz Patent-Motorwagen; thankfully he – and his wife Bertha – turned up, too. From then on it was all, well, not downhill, exactly, more... round and round in distorted circles.

Anyway. Back to that sepia past.

It's the year 1894. Herr Benz's motorcar has now been joined by many others, and no country is more enthusiastic for this new method of fast travel than France. Car manufacturers well understood the value of a competition that would show off their shiny new vehicles, and on the 22 July that year, Le Petit Journal, a Paris newspaper, organised the first 'official' race in the history of the Grand Prix. That first race also brought motor racing's first scandal. Zut alors! Well, a disqualification, in fact. The racetrack stretched for over 70 miles (126 kilometres) between Porte Maillot in Paris and Rouen. Having completed the course in six hours forty-eight minutes at an average, and mind-boggling, speed of 12 miles an hour (19.3 km/h), first over the line in Rouen was Count Jules-Albert de Dion. However, the count's car was steam driven and it needed a stoker to keep it fuelled. On account of this, the judges, who were looking for safety,

« Karl Benz

controllability and economy, disqualified the Count and ruled that second-placed Albert Lemaître, driving a Peugeot Type 7, 3hp, with his co-driver/mechanic Adolf Clemént-Bayard, a bicycle manufacturer, had taken first place. (There were joint winners, Auguste Doriot, René Panhard and Émile Levassor, as the cars were not judged on speed alone.) Albert had arrived at the finish line 3½ minutes behind de Dion.

(In fact, there was another, real scandal involving Albert, because in 1906, after his wife had filed for divorce, the two of them began an argument and Albert shot and killed her, before turning the gun on himself. The bullet to his head failed to kill him, however, and he was acquitted of a crime of passion.)

Nonetheless, motor racing was here to stay, and over the following years, motor races became a firm event in many French towns. Émile Levassor was evidently still a car enthusiast a year later, because in 1895 he won the race that year again, even though he was refused the FR. 31,000 prize because his car only had two seats instead of four. His drive was an extraordinary feat of endurance; he had hardly stopped during the 48 hours 48 minutes of his race. This 1895 event was notable for the fact that a certain André Michelin had entered the race in a car boasting pneumatic tyres. This newfangled invention must have caused a good few raised eyebrows amongst aficionados, because poor André suffered many humiliating punctures along the route. So they would obviously never catch on.

1895 was also the year that saw the formation of the Automobile Club de France (ACF), and the first race event ever held in Italy. Those thrilling and startling speeds of 9.6mph were achieved over a 57-mile (93km) course, but in the years to the end of the century, the search for increased speed gathered pace and 7 and 8-litre engines began to make their appearance.

It was an American, James Gordon Bennett, who wrote the next chapter in the history of motor racing. His father was the founder, editor and publisher of the New York Herald. Gordon junior was a sports enthusiast, who had been educated largely in France, and in 1866 he took over the New York Herald from his father. Gordon did not drive, yet in 1899, with a newspaperman's eye for publicity, he organised what came to be known as the Gordon Bennett Cup Race, six international races held annually between 1900 and 1906. France, Germany, Great Britain, Italy, the United States, Belgium, Switzerland, and Austria all competed. The cars had to have two side-by-side seats occupied by the driver and a mechanic. The first race – the average speed by now was a hair-raising 38.6 mph (62.1km/h) – was won by Fernand Charron driving a Panhard-Levassor (yes, you guessed correctly, the very same Monsieur Émile Levassor; although, sadly, he had died in 1897 following an automobile accident the previous year).

Cars lining up for the Gordon Bennett Cup in Paris, Bordeaux 29th May 1901

International colours were assigned to the competitors for the first time; blue for France, white for Germany, red to the USA, yellow for Belgium, with Britain (which first competed in 1902) choosing green and Italy only adopting its 'racing red' in 1907. Ireland hosted the race at Athy in 1903, and this was the first ever, closed-circuit race to take place, even though it was run over public roads.

But we're getting ahead of ourselves, slightly.

It was in 1901 that motor sport accelerated out of its infancy with the introduction of the 35hp Mercedes and a four-cylinder engine with mechanical valves and... zut alors, encore...! those hopeless pneumatic tyres, which were, of course, no longer hopeless. Having reached 35hp, however, the mechanics didn't stay there long, and the engine capacity of the Mercedes rapidly increased to 9 litres producing 60hp. The speeds rocketed accordingly; in the 1901 Gordon Bennett Cup race, the open Mors of Fournier reached an average speed of 53 mph (85.2 km/h).

That year is considered to be the birthday of the Grand Prix; the race that took place at Le Mans was the first to be described as a Grand Prix, and it was the Hungarian Ferencz Szisz driving a Renault, which boasted a 90hp engine, who raced into the history books by finishing first. He had covered the 700-mile course at

Léon Théry, winner of The Gordon Bennett Cup at the Circuit Auvergne Michelin on 5th July 1905

an average of 63 mph (101km/h).

Meanwhile, the Gordon Bennett Cup race was still going strong, and in 1903 in spectacular style, Camille Jenatzy created a sensation by driving with his foot down to the floor in a spine-tingling race that brought him the winner's cup and £8,000. Even more spectacular that year was the Paris-Bordeaux race; these were described as "fearsome, thrilling fights", but they claimed the lives of drivers and spectators alike, and in 1903, the French authorities called it a day. They stopped the race and confiscated the cars; it proved to be the last of the Paris–Bordeaux–Paris Trail Races that had begun in 1895, one of the classic city to city races in which drivers had hurtled between some of Europe's major capitals. By 1905, the Gordon Bennett Cup, too, had come to the end of its short life, and the finishing line was crossed for the last time in July that year in the Auvergne in central France. Victory went to the Frenchman Léon Théry, who won for the second year in a row in a 96hp Richard-Brasier, dashing round the course at an average speed of 48.3 mph (77.78 km/h).

That victory seemed to prove what every Frenchman already knew, that France was the leading motor racing country, and the French automobile industry, the largest in Europe, now wanted a competition to reflect this status. So, the AFC organised the Grand Prix for manufacturers on the 26 and 27 June 1906. But because so many drivers and spectators had already died during the sport's brief years of existence, organisers changed their ideas. This race would take place on a closed circuit, outside the city of Le Mans, along a route of 64.11 miles (103.18 kilometres). Each competitor would complete six laps over two days.

The race took place in heat so fierce it melted the tar of the roads, which was kicked up into the driver's faces, and those pneumatic tyres – there were some who still said "I told you so" – were continually getting punctures, although defective radiators and wheels were the biggest culprits in cars that failed to complete the course. There was a well-known face in the winning

Renault car, Ferenc Szisz, with Felice Nazzaro coming in second and another driver who was also well known by this time, Clément-Bayard, taking third place.

The race, ever afterwards to be known as the first Grand Prix, was not considered to have been as exciting as the Gordon Bennett Cup races, but, nonetheless, it was organised again in 1907 and inspired Germany to organise its own race that year, the Kaiserpreis, The Kaiser's Prize, which eventually became the German Grand Prix. 1907 was also the year in which the almost oval-shaped, steep banks of the Brooklands racetrack in England were completed.

So, the Grand Prix had firmly imprinted itself in the sporting calendar of Europe after just a decade on the roads. After a conference in 1904 it even had its own governing body, which had debated a French proposal for a change in format to the Gordon Bennett races; many national clubs then joined forces to found the Association Internationale des Automobile Clubs Reconnus, the AIACR, which later became the Fédération Internationale de l'Automobile, the regulating body for international motor sport.

In this exciting new age of motor racing, France lost its dominance and yielded space to the upstarts Alfa of Italy and especially Mercedes of Germany. From now on, spectators would be treated to a conveyor

The newly opened Brooklands in 1907

belt of new innovations and ever-faster cars. In 1908, shallow emplacements along the side of the track were introduced; the pit had made its appearance and was to be the scene of many a drama in the unfolding spectacle of the sport. The wheel, too, was undergoing a transformation. Although the pneumatic tyre had triumphed and replaced the old solid rubber one and a removable rim had facilitated faster removal of the wheel, the situation was far from satisfactory. In 1908, the Mercedes pit crew's work was made easier when they were given pneumatic jacks, and the cars were fitted with one-bolt wheels, a race-changing, revolutionary development; especially in those early years when tyres would be shredded by the poor road surfaces. Mercedes driver Christian Lautenschlager wrecked ten tyres before he raced over the line victorious that year.

The fierce nationalism involved in the races, let alone the commercial considerations, even at this early stage in the sport – winning manufacturers could expect a surge in sales from financing a winning team – and political wrangling, managed to prevent the Grand Prix from taking place between the years of 1909 and 1911. In the light of what was to come, this inability to allow even a motor race to overcome national pride was a bad omen. So the action moved to America, where the Indianapolis Motor Speedway was first used in 1909, and in 1911 there was another first; the Indianapolis 500-mile Race. Perhaps this galvanised the Grand Prix organisers into working together again, because in 1912, the Grand Prix was back up and running.

Peugeot had been busy refining their cars during the hiatus, and the results paid off immediately. These mighty cars are considered by many to have been the forerunners of the racing cars we know today, because thanks to engineer Ernest Henry, described as "... perhaps the most brilliant engine designer ever", a revolution in racing car technology had taken place; the latest Peugeot engines featured overhead valves inclined in the cylinder heads and operated by two overhead camshafts. It changed the world of racing from then on, and on June 25 and 26 1912, Georges Boillot won the Grand Prix in his Peugeot, after Fiat driver David Bruce-Brown had been disqualified for fuelling his car outside the pits. It was in this race that mechanic Jean Bassignano was killed when the wheel came off his and driver Léon Collinet's car in lap three and the car turned over.

The following year, with five fatalities before the race even started, Georges Boillot and Peugeot were triumphant once again, at Amiens, this time, averaging a speed of 72.141 mph (116.096 km/h). For that 1913 race, the Grand Prix cars had been restricted to a minimum weight of 1,764 lb (800 kg) and a maximum weight of 2,425 lb (1,100 kg), plus a fuel consumption limit of 14 mpg (20 l/100 km).

The Germans, however, had not been sitting 'idling'

Christian Lautenschlager

Indianapolis Motor Speedway poster, 1909

by as Peugeot went from strength to strength; far from it. They were back with a vengeance for the 1914 Grand Prix and lined up at the start at Lille on 4 July that year. Archduke Franz Ferdinand of Austria and his wife had been assassinated only a few days earlier on the 28 June and tension in Europe, especially between the French and Germans, was palpable.

This Grand Prix is regarded as being one of the greatest events in motor-racing history. Thirteen manufacturers from six different countries entered thirty-seven cars, and for the first time, a limit was set on the size of the engine allowed; 4.5 litres. A new feature of this race was that drivers were controlled by signals from the pit.

Eerily, the Grand Prix became a competition between the French Peugeot and the German Mercedes cars. The Germans dominated the race, despite Boillot taking the lead for twelve of the twenty laps, and the excitement of the 300,000 crowd of spectators was intense. By the time the French driver dropped out on the last lap, Ferenc Szisz, winner of the first Grand Prix, had been hit by a car whilst changing a wheel and broken his arm. The Mercedes cars passed the line in first, second and third places, with Christian Lautenschlager taking the winner's prize. The French onlookers were not pleased.

As the crowd dispersed and the excitement of the Grand Prix faded, there were more serious matters to think about, for within just a few weeks, Europe would be at war. Many of the drivers, the crews, and those admiring of their talents, would not return from the mighty conflict that claimed millions of lives. Amongst them was the driver Georges Boillot. He became a driver for the French Commander-in-Chief, General Joseph Joffre, before joining a flying unit and becoming an ace pilot. He won the Croix de Guerre and the Legion d'Honneur. On April the 21st 1916, engaged in a dogfight in which he shot down one of five German Fokkers attacking him, he was shot down, and crashed not far from Bar-le-Duc. He died on 19 May from his severe injuries, in Vadelaincourt military hospital in eastern France.

A sad, though courageous finalé, for a champion driver.

Christian Lautenschlager in his Mercedes at the 1908 French Grand Prix at Dieppe

THE INTER-WAR YEARS

During the war, some drivers had continued racing in America at the Indianapolis 500, and this tradition continued once the war had ended. Europe was shell-shocked, weary and devastated, and it was only in 1921 that the Grand Prix returned to excite European enthusiasts once more. But how would European car manufacturers fare after years of being out of the loop? The answer was, surprisingly well. Unsurprisingly, perhaps, an American Duesenberg, driven by Jimmy Murphy, was the first car over the line after 30 laps, having covered the course in four hours and seven minutes, with the Italian-American Ralph DePalma coming in second in his French Ballot, fifteen minutes behind. (Édouard Ballot was a well-known engine designer, who helped Ettore Bugatti develop his first engines.)

The 1920s ushered in exhilarating developments in the world of Grand Prix racing. The first Grand Prix competition held outside France took place in Italy in 1921, and it was followed in later years by Spain, Belgium, and then Britain in 1926. And changes in the sport were not only happening in the field of car design and engine construction. New circuits were being constructed all over Europe that were much shorter in length; the 1921 Italian Grand Prix was held on one of these. In 1922, the Commission Sportive Internationale (CSI) was given the

Henry Segrave and Jimmy Murphy at the 1921 French Grand Prix

Jimmy Murphy at the 1921 French Grand Prix

authority to regulate Grand Prix racing on behalf of the AIACR. That same year, a 2-litre engine capacity limit was introduced, so it was back to the drawing board for the designers.

One name, one engine design, began a short domination of Grand Prix racing for the second half of that decade, one of those names that sets motor enthusiasts' hearts beating a little faster; Ettore Bugatti. With drivers such as Louis Chiron and Tazio Nuvolari at the wheel, Bugatti swept the board every year for five consecutive years between 1925 and 1929 in the Targa Florio in the hills around Palermo in Sicily, Italy. The surge began in 1926; in 1927 they won twenty-three of thirty-one races, and the success continued throughout 1928 before slowing in 1929 and ebbing with the arrival of the thirties. When questioned about his dubious braking system, Bugatti is quoted as saying, "I build my cars to go, not stop". That he certainly did. It was a phenomenal achievement attained with beautifully designed bodywork as well, and the Bugatti Type 35 went on to become one of the most successful cars in history. It was developed by Bugatti and Jean Chassagne, his master engineer and a racing driver, who also drove the Bugatti for the Type 35's first ever Grand Prix, in Lyon in 1924.

"The road holding was fantastic… the precision of the steering was something fantastic", said one of the men who got behind the wheel in 1930, René Dreyfus. It was envied by all.

Staggered starts became a thing of the past, too, abandoned in 1922 in favour of the mass start, which made its debut in the French Grand Prix in Strasbourg. In 1925 came another major change; and not for the first time it was brought about because of a death on the track. The English mechanic Tom Barrett was riding in a Sunbeam car – the first British car to win a Grand Prix race, incidentally – with driver Kenelm Lee Guinness, for the San Sebastian Grand Prix in 1924. On lap eleven, Guinness's car hit a rut, spun around and tipped over, throwing the two occupants into a railway cutting. Tom Barrett was killed instantly. In shock, Guinness never raced again. It was a moment of decision for the sport. No longer would mechanics be allowed to ride in a Grand Prix car. Tom Barrett's tragedy undoubtedly saved the lives of many future mechanics.

Mercedes-Benz were again responsible for innovation, this time off the track, when they introduced a system of flags and boards to relate tactical information to their drivers. It had been invented by their racing manager Alfred Neubauer. They tried out this system in the 1926 Solituderennen near Stuttgart in Germany.

By 1928, the strict 'formula' of restrictions on engine size and vehicle weight that had guided the Grand Prix races since their inception, were all but discarded, heralding an era that became known as Formula Libre; as the name indicated, there were practically no limitations for these competitions. One year later, the number of Grand Prix competitions had increased, so at the beginning of a new decade, motor racing was in a healthy situation. One proof of this was the

Ettore Bugatti

introduction of the AIACR European Championship in 1931; for the record, it was won by Ferdinando Minoia driving for the Alfa Corse team.

When the drivers lined up at the start of the Monaco Grand Prix of 1933, they had taken part in qualifying laps for the first time, so that the fastest qualifying speed would be rewarded by a pole position on the grid. Racing was gradually taking a shape familiar to the modern world.

The early years of the thirties were in the grip of the Great Depression. Understandably, interest in motor racing declined somewhat. Nevertheless, the racetrack produced a legendary driver, the Italian Tazio Nuvolari, "Il Mantovano Volante", "The Flying Mantuan", whose victories in his Alfa Romeo were thrilling to watch. European Champion in 1932, then during a two-year hiatus in the European Championship, he won seven Grands Prix in 1933. In 1935, he was triumphant in a four-year-old Alfa Romeo against nine German cars. Without doubt, one of the greatest drivers of his day; no less a person than Auto Union designer Dr. Ferdinand Porsche said so and he should know. Nuvolari changed to Auto Union (later Audi) in 1938.

With Hitler ensconced in power in Germany, a new nationalism had been injected into the country, and Mercedes and Auto Union were being encouraged to build ever more sophisticated cars to prove the superiority of German craftsmanship. And the two teams didn't let the Führer down. Well, you wouldn't, would you? Initially producing sleek, aerodynamic machines that could exceed 175 mph (Mercedes would develop cars with 600bhp and top speeds reaching 200 mph before the decade was out), between 1935 and 1939 they dominated the European Grand Prix finish line, claiming

The 1933 Monaco Grand Prix, with drivers skidding around the tricky Fairmont hairpin

a host of championships; there were eighteen Grands Prix by 1934. The Auto Union cars boasted V16 4.4-litre supercharged engines requiring special fuels concocted according to highly secret formulae. A four-wheel independent suspension used by both cars, was then swopped by Mercedes for a De Dion system, with rear leaf springs later being replaced by a torsion-bar suspension.

This was the golden age of the mighty 'Silberpfeile', the 'Silver Arrows', the nickname given to the German cars in 1934 because the aluminium body had been left unpainted to reduce the weight. Legend has it that they were 1.656 lb (1 kg) too heavy, and both Alfred Neubauer, the racing manager, and driver Manfred von Brauchitsch claimed the idea as their own. Fame is, indeed, a seductive lady. Manfred von Brauchitsch, Hermann Lang and Rudolf Caracciola were the drivers who could always be seen behind the wheel of a Silberpfeil in those heady years that produced some of the greatest cars ever made, with one of Britain's greatest pre-war drivers, Richard Seaman, getting a look in on three occasions, too. In fact, to the great delight of the German fans, he took the Silberpfeil to victory in the German Grand Prix in 1938. Tragedy awaited Seaman, however, because in 1939 during the Belgian Grand Prix, he crashed his car into a tree. The engine burst into flames and the unconscious driver was so badly burned, that he died of his injuries just a few hours later. Reading of his death becomes unbearably poignant when we are told that his last words were; "I was going too fast for the conditions – it was entirely my own fault. I am sorry". He was just 26 years old.

Grand Prix motor racing is, indeed, an unforgiving mistress.

With the war to end all wars still vivid in the memory, a few people now decided that sending people off to fight was even more exciting than motor racing, so everyone drained their beers and went off to slaughter each other again.

Motor racing in Europe came to standstill once more, in 1939.

As in WWI, many drivers didn't return to their cars after the conflict ended; amongst them were Jean Trenoulet, a French resistance fighter, who died on the 13th October 1944, Luis Fontés, who died on the 12th of October 1940 when his Wellington crashed, Ulli Bigalke, who died in his Luftwaffe plane, André Embiricos, who died on the 23rd of May 1941, killed during a naval battle off Crete and Ernst Günther Burggaller, killed in an accident in his Messerschmitt on the 2nd of February 1940.

»

Auto Union driver Bernd Rosemeyer [#16] trails Rudolf Caracciola in his 'Silver Arrows' Mercedes in a 1936 race

A BRIEF PERIOD OF ADJUSTMENT

Miraculously, in 1945, having seen their factories first of all converted to military production and then heavily bombed during the war years, car manufacturers began motor racing on the Continent again in September 1945. And once again, it was car-crazy France that took the lead, so to speak, organising three races along a circuit in the Bois de Boulogne in Paris. Fittingly, the initial competition was a memorial race for a trophy named after Robert Benoist, a driver for Bugatti before the war, who had been shot by the Gestapo in 1944. (Benoist, and two other drivers, William Grover-Williams and Jean-Pierre Wimille, joined the Special Operations Executive (SOS) as secret agents. Grover-Williams was also executed.)

1927, Robert Benoist in his Delage after his victory at Monza

The races were won by a hybrid Simca/Fiat, a Maserati, and there was a highly emotional win, for the spectators and Jean-Pierre Wimille, who had had surged forwards, unstoppable, in a 4.7-litre Bugatti T59. Is it too sentimental to believe that he was determined to win, as a memorial to his SOE friends? Whatever the reason, Benoist and Grover-Williams would have been proud of him.

Those post-war years were glory years for the Italian cars, with Maserati and Alfa Romeo powering around the circuits and boasting some of the great names in racing at the wheels of their masterpieces of engineering; Alberto Ascari, Luigi Villoresi, and, of course, the inimitable Juan Manuel Fangio. These years also

The 1946 French Grand Prix

brought forth classic, wheel to wheel contests between the great cars of the day, Maserati, Ferrari, Talbot and Alfa Romeo, and they were the years in which spectators could delight in the feverish activity at the regular fuelling stops, which had by now been honed to a fine art and were all over in twenty seconds or less.

Leaving the war years behind them, the racing fraternity formed The Fédération Internationale d'Automobiles (FIA) to organise international motor racing events, and in 1947 the formula agreed upon permitted 1.5-litre supercharged or 4.5-litre non-supercharged cars. As the decade progressed, one by one the old Grand Prix tracks were put back into order; in Italy in 1947, the Italian Grand Prix was held at Milan until it could finally return to its Monza home in 1949. The German Grand Prix returned to the Nürburgring in 1950 once the damage caused by the American 11th Armored Division tanks had been repaired.

1947 also brought with it a major change in the regulation of the Grand Prix competition. In that year, the formalisation of the World Drivers' Championship was agreed; several of the national Formula One Grands Prix would form the basis of a World Championship for drivers. Although three more years were to pass before the first official race took place, F1 regulations were followed from then on.

The 1940s bade farewell to a legendary car maker when Ettore Bugatti died in a Parisian military hospital from a lung infection on August 21 1947; but the decade said hello to what was to become an equally famous name in 1948, when Enzo Ferrari, who in 1929 had started his own firm, Scuderia Ferrari, entered the Grand Prix fray, winning the Circuito di Garda in October. The following year, 1949, the Ferrari crossed the line in first place on four occasions, stating firmly that here was a name to watch. It was in an open Ferrari 166C in 1948 that the legendary driver Tazio Nuvolari drove the race that endeared him to everyone and had Enzo Ferrari, with tears in his eyes, pleading with the seriously ill driver to quit as his car fell to pieces around him. Undaunted, only a broken spring prevented Nuvolari from gaining a spectacular victory. He had been part of, and now he witnessed the end of, an extraordinary epoch of motor racing.

As the 1950s dawned, so, too, did a thrilling new chapter in the story of Grand Prix racing.

The Ferrari (#36) driven by Igor Troubetzkoy leads the Talbot of Yves Giraud-Cabantous in the 1948 Monaco Grand Prix

Stirling Moss of Great Britain being wished good luck by his father, former Brooklands driver Alfred Moss before taking part in the 250 mile Grand Prix race at Silverstone. It was the first recognised Grand Prix in Britain since before the Second World War and Stirling Moss was the youngest driver in the 500 cc race, 2nd October 1948

Avid racer Prince Bira of Siam in a Maserati cornering at the Dutch Grand Prix, Zandvoort 1948

A British ERA, driven by G Ansell during a spectacular mid-air crash at Silverstone Grand Prix ciruit, October 1948

THE PIONEER RACERS

Before the advent of Formula One in 1950, early motorsport was blessed with a series of trailblazing racers who paved the way for today's modern Grand Prix stars.

Ferenc Szisz

The first race to bear the Grand Prix moniker was organised by the Automobile Club de France (ACF) and was staged in 1906 at Le Mans. The man to claim victory in the historic event was Hungarian Szisz, one of 32 drivers representing 12 different manufacturers, who was fastest over two days and almost 770 miles of gruelling high-speed action. With his mechanic alongside with him in the passenger seat of his Renault AK 90CV, the 32-year-old's victorious time for the event was over 12 hours, some 32 minutes faster than runner-up Felice Nazzaro of Italy in a Fiat. "I feared something small which would take away victory at the moment when it had seemed to be won," Szisz said on the podium after his famous French Grand Prix triumph. The Hungarian raced in only three further GPs in his career, the fourth and last time in 1914, but his place in embryonic motorsport history was already assured.

Antonio Ascari

The father of future two-time Formula One world champion Alberto, Ascari Senior was one of the leading lights in the first season of the World Manufacturers' Championship, motorsport's first recognised global competition which ran for five years from 1925. The Italian was one of the five drivers who helped secure the inaugural championship title for Alfa Romeo, winning the Belgium Grand Prix at Spa-Francorchamps. The winner of the Italian Grand Prix the previous year and a noted engineering innovator, Ascari at the age of 36 was killed just a month after his Belgian triumph while heading the field at the French Grand Prix at the Autodrome

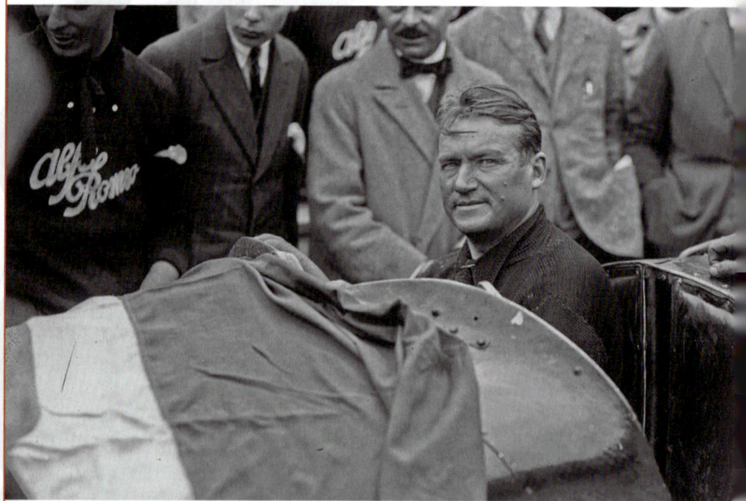

de Montlhéry. His car hit a fence while navigating a corner and he later succumbed to his injuries in an ambulance en route to hospital. His body was laid out in the Alfa Romeo HQ in Milan, where thousands paid their final respects.

Tazio Nuvolari

Described by the legendary Ferdinand Porsche as "the greatest driver of the past, the present, and the future", Nuvolari began his racing career on two rather than four wheels but by the 1930s had graduated from motorbikes to Grands Prix. His first season in the European Championship in 1931 saw 'The Flying

Mantuan' finish fifth with Alfa Corse, Alfa Romeo's factory team, but the following year he left all challengers in his wake, winning in his native Italy and France to become a pre-Formula One 'world champion'. In 1933 Nuvolari, who also drove for Ferrari and later Auto Union, triumphed at the 24 Hours of Le Mans and featured in every edition of the European Championship until the Second World War brought it to an abrupt halt after 1939. Nuvolari registered 24 Grand Prix wins overall, the only major omission on his impressive CV being the Czechoslovakian GP.

Richard Seaman

One of British motorsport's early trailblazers, Seaman's racing career was tragically short but in his brief time on the Grand Prix stage he indelibly wrote his name into the record books. His unforgettable moment came at

the German Grand Prix, staged at the iconic Nürburgring, during the 1938 European Championship season as his Mercedes W125 outpaced his rivals to the delight of Silver Arrows fans. It was to be his only success with the famed German giant and in 1939 the 26-year-old's life was cut short when his car caught fire during the Belgian Grand Prix after a collision with a tree. During his fleeting career, Seaman made seven European Championship starts, registering two podium finishes and two fastest laps before his untimely death at Spa-Francorchamps.

Rudolf Caracciola

Dubbed by 'Regenmeister' (or 'Rainmaster') in his native Germany in a nod to his mastery of wet conditions, Caracciola fractured his thigh in 1933 during practice for the Monaco Grand Prix. The injury kept him off the track for over a year but he returned for the newly formed Mercedes team for the 1935 edition of the European Championship. It was a spectacular return to the fray with his four GP victories in seven races sealing motorsport's unofficial world title for the German. He was off the pace 12 months later but Caracciola bounced back, claiming the crown again in 1937 and 1938, to become the only man to register a hat-trick of European Championship triumphs. He also remains the most successful driver in German Grand Prix history, winning the famous race six times between 1926 and 1939, eclipsing the subsequent efforts of four-time winners Michael Schumacher and Lewis Hamilton.

In the wake of the end of the Second World War, motorsport came together and modern, global Formula One was born. Despite its European roots, the first decade of breakneck racing was dominated by Argentina's dashing star Juan Manuel Fangio, as 'El Maestro' etched his name into history

FORMULA ONE COMES OF AGE

1950-69

Fangio leading the chasing pack in his Mercedes, with his teammate and rival Stirling Moss in his slipstream at the Dutch Grand Prix, 1955

The 1950 Grand Prix season, which included the inaugural FIAA World Championship of Drivers, began on 13 May and ended on 3 September. This would be a spectacular year for Alfa Romeo, as they won all six of the European Grands Prix. The points system initially gave eight points to the winner of each qualifying round, six to the second-placed car, four to the third, three for the fourth, two for the fifth and an extra point for the driver of the fastest lap. Ferrari had decided to use un-supercharged engines that year, and Aurelio Lampredi produced a 12-cylinder Ferrari that developed 300bhp at 7300rpm. Ferrari made their World Championship debut at the Monaco Grand Prix, but the decision to change engines had no impact on the championship table, because it was Alfa Romeo who homed in on championship victory with Guiseppe Farina at the wheel. Alfa took the championship again in 1951. The driver this time was to dominate the Grands Prix of the 1950s from then on; his name was Juan Manuel Fangio. An Argentinean nicknamed, 'El Maestro', Fangio is still revered and considered by many to be the greatest driver of all time. It was Fangio's last race behind the wheel of an Alfa, and it was the year that Ferrari's technical developments began to reap rewards; they won three victories that year – Alfa won four – and those wins signalled the end of track dominance by Ferrari's arch rival.

Fangio's last race of the season, to take the championship for the first time, took place at the Spanish Grand Prix, and it was Alfa Romeo's decision to use 18-inch tyres that won the day. Ferrari had chosen 16 inch... and spent a great deal of the race changing tyres because of tread problems. As a result, Fangio won with relative ease.

So few people had registered for the Formula 1 races that it was decided to run Formula 2 competitions in 1952 and 1953 instead; Formula 2 rules limited engines to 2-litre naturally aspirated, or 750cc supercharged cars. The steering of those racing cars in the early 1950s was still heavy and imprecise and therefore demanded great strength from a driver. A momentary

Argentine Juan Manuel Fangio

miscalculation, or an irregular engine stroke in a bend, would instantly have the car in a spin. But developments were taking place continuously, and in 1951, one of the new technological advancements was introduced at Indianapolis; the revolutionary disc brake system. On the road, the style that drivers used to take corners as fast as they could involved no brakes at all, if possible, and was known as the "four wheel drift". The driver would adopt a slightly longitudinal angle to the corner and as the wheels began to lose traction on the road surface they would be controlled by throttle and steering alone.

Ferrari took the limelight in spectacular fashion the following year, banishing Alfa from the podium completely and sweeping the Grand Prix board. They almost achieved the same feat in 1953, again with Alberto Ascari at the wheel, winning all but one of the European Grands Prix, yielding just the final race of the season at Monza in Italy to Fangio, now driving a Maserati.

And for the next four seasons, Fangio was the man you wanted behind the wheel of your car. If he was, you would be victorious and Ferrari, Maserati and Mercedes drove victorious Grands Prix with him ensconced in their shining automobiles. It was an extraordinary achievement by the Argentinean; five championships, a record only broken by Michael Schumacher forty-seven years later. Fangio was ten years older than the German driver would be when the record was broken.

That final race of 1953 in Monza announced the return of Fangio to the top of the class. It started off as a four-way struggle between Fangio, Ascari, Farina and Onofre Marimón. (Sadly, Marimón would become the first driver to be fatally injured at a Grand Prix World Championship, when he was killed on 31 July 1954 during a practice run for the German Grand Prix.) For 46 laps, these four were never more than twenty metres apart, and there were twenty-six changes of leader. The final lap was one of those breath-taking finishes that motor racing can deliver to the spectators, five drivers hurtling down the track together with Fangio behind Ascari and Farina as they approached the last corner. Overtaking and under pressure, Ascari suddenly spun out of control at the last corner, and Farina, in the effort to avoid him, ran onto the grass. Fangio, with lightening reactions, darted through unscathed and shot over the finish line. Ascari became

The start of the 1953 Dutch Grand Prix

the Grand Prix winner for the second consecutive year with 34.5 points. Fangio in second place had 28; a new motor-racing hero was soaring upwards.

Incidentally, a young Englishman driving a Cooper Alta came in unceremoniously at number thirteen that year. He would later be described as "the greatest driver never to win the World Championship". His name? Stirling Moss.

The reign of un-supercharged 2500cc cars arrived in 1954. Fangio had been hired by the feared Silver Arrows team of Daimler-Benz, but their powerful giants didn't appear until July the 4th that year, so he began by driving the Maserati. He was immediately successful in the first two Grand Prix of the season in Argentina and Belgium. In July, the new W196, eight-cylinder Mercedes-Benz cars were available and three of them lined up for the start, with Fangio in one of them, accompanied by Karl Kling and Hans Herrmann in the other two. It must have been an imposing, if not fearful sight for the other drivers. And they had reason to be worried, because even though Herrmann managed to over rev his engine and blow it up on lap seventeen, (by which time Mike Hawthorn had also blown up his Ferrari engine) by then, he had broken the lap record. Fangio and Kling had smoothly gone to the front. And there they stayed, side by side, battling for the lead all the way to the finishing line where the team ordered Kling to take second place. Thus, Fangio won a punishing race in which only six cars finished. British driver Mike Hawthorn, in fact, came third in the table that year, but Fangio had streamed away to win the championship with 42 points. Fangio won all except the Spanish Grand Prix, in which he had been beaten by Mike Hawthorn putting in one of the best performances of his career in his Ferrari. It was a thrilling duel between the two of them, until loss of oil finally defeated Fangio. Maserati, Ferrari and Mercedes; these were the almost unbeatable teams of the 1950s;

«

Stirling Moss

Mercedes won twice, Ferrari four times and Maserati also won twice between 1952 and 1959.

This fierce competition meant that there was much to look forward to in the 1955 season. Stirling Moss was now Fangio's teammate at Mercedes alongside Kling and Herrmann. Everyone anticipated a great contest with Grands Prix that would have them on the tips of their toes.

It turned out to be a year of horrific tragedies, one of the worst seasons the sport has ever known.

American driver and double winner of the Indianapolis, Bill Vukovich was killed in May; another American, Manny Ayulo, had died just two weeks before. The celebrated Italian driver Alberto Ascari died testing sports cars at Monza, having ignored the warning when he had crashed into the harbour at Monaco four days earlier. His death was so upsetting it caused the Lancia team to close down their motor racing enterprise, and all their equipment was handed to Ferrari. On June 11 at the Le Mans 24-hour race, an even worse disaster struck. Mike Hawthorn had slowed down as he cut into the pits in his Jaguar D-Type, forcing Lance Macklin in his Austin Healey 100 to take evasive action and swerve, which kicked up a dust cloud and put him into the path of Pierre Levegh's Mercedes. Levegh had no time to react. He struck the Austin Healey at 150 mph (240 km/h) and the Mercedes scythed up into the air before hitting a retaining embankment and disintegrating. Chunks of metal and engine parts burst into the air and were hurled into the onlookers, and when Levegh was thrown from his car, his skull was crushed on impact with the ground and he was killed. As the magnesium-rich metal alloys ignited, white-hot flames swallowed the Mercedes, and the result of the conflagration and the shrapnel effect of the metal resulted in eighty-three spectators being killed and over one hundred injured.

The French, German, Swiss and Spanish Grands Prix were cancelled, before Fangio finally claimed his championship having won four of the six races. He never raced at Le Mans again. The sport was banned, and is

Fangio and Moss, teammates at Mercedes in 1955

Alberto Ascari

still banned, in Switzerland, and the Pedralbes course in Spain was never used again.

The tragic veil thrown over the season rather overshadowed a thrilling success for one man. Stirling Moss beat Fangio, to the delight of the home crowd, in the British Grand Prix on 16 July. Moss had also driven the fastest round in 2.00.4. Fangio always maintained that Moss had simply been the better driver on the day.

A final consequence of this appalling season was that Mercedes followed Lancia's example and withdrew from motor sport but for an unspecified time. The highly successful and advanced engineering of the Mercedes constructors, fifteen Grand Prix cars in the Formula One period with twelve first places in fifteen races in two Formula One seasons, would not be revived in circuit racing until the 1980's. Only in 2010 did Mercedes GP enter the F1 table again as an independent team with Nico Rosberg at the wheel, although in 1998 a McLaren-Mercedes car would send Mika Häkkinen across the finishing line, victorious again.

With considerable relief and hopes for a better year in 1956, the German team's achievements were overshadowed, with a strong showing by British cars such as the Connaught Alta GP 2.5 L4 and the Vanwall 254 2.5 L4, driven by Colin Chapman and Mike Hawthorn amongst others. Mike Hawthorn also drove a BRM Type 25; it was very fast, the four-cylinder engine developed 270bhp at 8000rpm and it sported disc brakes, but suffered from beginner's bad luck. Fangio was now with Ferrari, and Stirling Moss had moved on to Maserati, with

Ferraris 801 cars driven by Mike Hawthorn and Peter Collins at the Nürburgring in the 1957 German Grand Prix

British Vanwall at Aintree in 1957

whom he twice took victories from Fangio and ran the fastest lap three times over the season. With Fangio's teammate, the British driver Peter Collins, taking first place in two more races – one of which, the Belgian GP, riveted spectators with its wheel to wheel duel between Moss and Fangio – only Ferrari and Maserati got a look in this year. Fangio took a record third consecutive championship although with the least number of points he had ever attained, 30.

Those British Vanwalls provided some stirling opposition – yes, as you are asking, I did have to get that one in – in 1957, the season when Fangio won his fifth consecutive World Championship, this time in a Maserati. The British unleashed a formidable three-man team this year; Stirling Moss, Tony Brooks, and Stuart Lewis-Evans; what a team it was. Time and again it was Stirling Moss in his Vanwall who engaged the champion in the most nail-biting races of the season, robbing the Argentinean of three victories. But the excitement got to them on occasion: Moss was leading in the Monaco race but only got as far as the fourth lap before taking a chicane too fast and slamming into the barriers. His two British teammates seemed to think that Moss was enjoying some fun without them and promptly did exactly the same thing, removing all three cars from the race in one go. Taking the sense of British fair play a little too far, perhaps? That left the way open for Fangio to take another victory. That race was also notable for the interesting finish by an Australian driver, who would make his name in later years, to take sixth position; Jack Brabham had to push his Cooper Climax T43 over the finish line when his car developed a blockage in the petrol tank. He wouldn't have to wait long for his moment in the sun, though.

Jack Brabham

All those who know anything about motor racing accept that that the Grand Prix in Germany turned out to be the greatest race in Fangio's extraordinary career. And as fate would have it, he battled for supremacy in the race that would make history, against the young British drivers Mike Hawthorn and Peter Collins in Ferrari 801s. For Fangio, it would prove to be the race of his life in his Maserati 250 F. He chose to start off with a half-full tank and soft tyres, and the pit stop almost proved to be his undoing when the wheel nut rolled beneath the car and couldn't be found for thirty agonising seconds. He finally emerged forty-eight seconds behind Collins, who was in second place. Not only did he catch up to Hawthorn, he overtook him on the twenty-first lap, and in the course of a fierce battle with him, in which Fangio was almost overtaken, he broke the lap record nine times. Nine times! And Collins had already set a new lap record of 9 minutes 28.9 seconds. By the end of the race, Fangio had reduced that to 9 minutes 17.4 seconds. It was an extraordinary feat of driving. The Argentinean knew that his had been an astounding victory. After the race he said, "I have never driven that quickly before in my life and I don't think I will ever be able to do it again... I had never before had the courage to push things so far". A tribute, too, therefore, directed at the two British drivers who had inspired his magnificent win. Fittingly, Hawthorn and Collins came in second and third with Stirling Moss in fifth position. It had been a good day for the British cars and drivers. They had staked their claim and would not long remain without victory. And for the first time since the start of the series, Ferrari did not win a single World Championship race that year.

If 1957 had been a year of superlatives for Fangio, 1958 must go down in the annals of British racing history as one of the most extraordinary ever. Looking at the table of GP winners for that year, there were only two non-British drivers in the list, the American Jimmy Bryan and French driver Maurice Trintignant, and even he won the Monaco Grand Prix in a British Cooper Climax. Holland, Belgium, France, Morocco, they fell like dominos before the mighty British wave as Stirling Moss, Mike Hawthorn, Peter Collins, Roy Salvadori and Tony Brooks swept all aside that dared challenge them. They occupied the first five places in the championship table, with the American Harry Schell on joint fifth.

The incomparable Juan Manuel Fangio, the man that everyone praised as a driver and for his character, retired following the French Grand Prix in July, probably understanding that his day was over and new lions were on the prowl.

One of those lions was, in fact, a lioness, Maria Teresa de Filippis. She was born in Italy on 11 November 1926 and on 18 May 1958 she made Grand Prix history by being the first woman to race in Formula One. She eventually participated in five World Championship Grands Prix.

The International Cup for F1 Manufacturers was awarded for the first time in 1958 – Vanwall won that inaugural Constructors' Championship – and although the formula for the engines was left unchanged, one major difference had been the reduction of maximum race lengths to 186 miles (300 km) or two hours, whichever came first. Specialised, alcohol-based racing fuels had been replaced because commercial petrol had become compulsory.

Even though Stirling Moss took four victories that year, he lost out by one point in the championship, to Mike Hawthorn, who brought home Britain's first World

Championship title. The racing world was stunned by this British blockbusting performance. The Italians, in particular, must have wondered if they had woken up on another planet from the one they'd been on previously. Success had been achieved through one brilliant piece of design in construction; the British constructors had placed the engine in the centre of the car with the fuel tanks on either side, which rendered the car more responsive to the steering. Being able to dispense with the driveshaft meant not only a saving in weight, but it also enabled the driver to be positioned lower in the car and so improve the aerodynamics of the car body.

But it seemed as if the gods of fortune had decided that the glamorous young British lions were enjoying more than their fair share of glory. Tragedy had struck.

Blond and handsome, the epitome of a young athlete, Peter Collins, who, in the British Grand Prix less than two weeks before had taken victory in front of his jubilant home crowd, was killed in an accident at the German Nürburgring on August 3 when his Ferrari ran wide, left the track, hit a ditch and somersaulted on the eleventh lap. On 19 October during the Moroccan Grand Prix, Stuart Lewis-Evans lost control of the car when his Vanwall engine seized and he careered into a barrier where the car burst into flames. He died from his burns a week later.

Luigi Mosso, Hawthorn's great rival, was also killed in 1958. He, too, had gone wide on a corner and hit a ditch, sending his Ferrari into a somersault.

Barely was the new year of 1959 underway before Mike Hawthorn was taken, killed in a road accident near London on 22 January. All the more poignant because only a few days before, the new World Champion had announced that at the age of 29, he was retiring from racing, still devastated by the death of his good friend Peter Collins the year before.

There was a new name in the game in 1959; the first United States Grand Prix took place at the Sebring International Raceway near Florida; it was won by New Zealander Bruce McLaren at the age of twenty-two; the youngest ever winner in Grand Prix history, a record that endured for almost five decades.

Stirling Moss adjusts the helmet of Mike Hawthorn in his Ferrari before a race in 1958

A young Bruce McLaren at Oulton Park circuit UK, in 1959

But the big news of the year was that Jack Brabham's hour had finally arrived, and with him, the car that would change motor racing, the rear-engined Cooper Climax T51. And he took the World Championship in 1959 even though he only won two races, with 31 points. He also made history when he ran out of fuel 500 yards from the line in the last race of the season at the American Sebring circuit and pushed his car over the finishing line.

Only Maurice Trintignant amongst the top drivers managed to complete every race. Aston Martin entered its DBR4/1 for the first time that year, but its designers seem to have been asleep because it was already out of date by the time it got to the track.

Jack Brabham took the championship again in 1960, this time not so much by default, but by superb driving in his Cooper-Climax T53, winning five of the Grands Prix, yielding just two victories to Stirling Moss in his Lotus-Climax, with another one going to American Phil Hill in his Ferrari, and one to Bruce McLaren. Two notable incidents that year were that John Surtees, a motorcycle champion, had tried his hand at motor racing in the British Grand Prix, coming in second, and Stirling Moss had been badly injured in a practice accident in which his half-shaft failed; the accident prevented him from competing in many more races that year. Just a quick mention that on the technical side, 1960 saw the end

of the 2.5-litre Formula One, and the front-engined Formula One car was relegated to racing history.

With the winning driver now awarded ten points, Ferrari raced back to victory the following season, although it proved a rare exception to a trend that had already started and would continue; the predominance of British-manufactured winning cars. The Italians swept the board that year losing out on just three races, to win their first F1 constructor's title. Their driver, Phil Hill, won the Championship with 34 points, the first American to do so. His teammate, Wolfgang von Trips, had won two races, had 33 points, and needed just third place to win the championship before he was killed in the penultimate race in Italy; an accident that also took the lives of fifteen spectators. Von Trips had hit the car driven by an up and coming young British driver.

Scotland's Jim Clark burst into the public's consciousness in 1962, when the Grand Prix season became a fierce duel between Clark and England's Graham Hill. Ferrari were once again wiped off the motor racing map; by Clark's Lotus-Climax 25 and Hill's BRM P56, and the two drivers shared seven victories between them with only Bruce McLaren and Dan Gurney managing to squeeze in one win apiece. But this was to be Graham Hill's World Championship, the man who had only passed his driving test at the age of 24. Hill's

Jack Brabham in a Cooper Climax T55 at the La Source hairpin in the Belgian Grand Prix Spa-Francorchamps, 1961

son Damon, would many years later also take a Grand Prix championship, making them the only father and son ever to do so, although his father was sadly no longer alive when Damon became World Champion. Amongst the celebrations in the British camp there was also a sense of sadness when it was announced that Stirling Moss would retire from racing. He had been badly injured in a serious crash at Goodwood and had required surgery. He recovered. Nonetheless, his eyesight had suffered, and he realised that he would never again achieve his former speed of reaction. A whole series of unfortunate incidents had denied Moss a World Championship that for a driver of his calibre should, by any criteria, have been his.

Jim Clark and Graham Hill in battle, 1963

Jim Clark. The good-looking young Scot was now to see his bravery rewarded, and the measure of his World Championship win in 1963 can be taken by the fact that he had won the title by the end of his seventh race, out of a total of ten. It was another extraordinary season for the British, in fact; for the drivers, Clark and Hill it was almost a complete British whitewash. The only non-British team to cross the finishing line ahead of the other drivers was Ferrari, once, and even that car was driven by John Surtees.

The season was a more dramatic repeat of the previous one, with Clark and Hill battling each other for supremacy; but this time the roles were reversed. Graham Hill won the first race of the season. On his second outing, however, Clark showed what he was made of. In appallingly wet and rainy conditions and having started eighth on the grid, Clark had overtaken the entire field by lap seventeen, and he won the race 4.54 minutes ahead of Bruce McLaren in second place, as though he'd been driving through brilliant sunshine. Clark

Jim Clark

John Surtees in his Ferrari ahead of Dan Gurney, 1964

went on to take the championship with seven victories to Graham Hill's two, and John Surtees' single victory in his V6 Ferrari Type 156B in Germany. It was an astonishing season for the young Clark, who had become the first driver to win the Drivers' World Championship with three races still to go. Only in 1984 did Alain Prost equal Clark's record sequence of victories.

The Ferrari engineers must have breathed a sigh of relief the following year; finally, they were back in force with winning cars. Still, they didn't have it all their own way; the Brits were not going to give up without a fight, and Lotus, the new Brabhams as well as BRM, gave them a run for their money in a truly exciting four-way race. Jim Clark again won most races, three, with Graham Hill, John Surtees and the American Dan Gurney hot on his heels with two each.

When they arrived for the Mexican Grand Prix on October 25 1964, the drivers lined up for a finalé that thrilled spectators as one of the most riveting in Grand Prix history. Three drivers were in with a chance of victory; Graham Hill, Jim Clark and John Surtees. Surtees struggled for a long time on fifth place, but Hill's chances were severely curtailed when he was rear ended and spun around, although he managed to get back into the race. And then more bad luck, for Clark this time. With sixty of the sixty-five laps covered, Clark's engine lost oil and began to seize. On the penultimate lap he lost the lead, and when Surtees' teammate Bandini was ordered to allow Surtees over the line ahead of him into second place, Surtees had won his first, his only, World Championship. Clark was fifth in Mexico and Hill eleventh.

In the midst of all this drama, a young driver was sneaking up quietly on his peers; his name was Jochen Rindt. As it had for Clark, fame would soon come to the young German, too. But Clark had to be beaten first, and he who had been robbed in 1964 flared back to glory in

Graham Hill

9
TEAM LOTUS
TEAM LOTUS

1965. And he began the challenge for his second World Championship, by not competing in the second Formula One race, the Monaco Grand Prix, driving instead in the Indianapolis 500.

Lotus worked in tandem with the Ford Motor Company to produce a car in which Clark became the first European in nearly five decades to win this prestigious American race. The Lotus was a monocoque Type 38 with a Ford V8 motor that developed 495bhp at 8800rpm. The wider tyres now used on Grand Prix cars boasted just over 200mm surface contact, which was considered the optimum amount when paired with the smaller wheel radius. With the linings now made of nylon, the days of shredded rubber were far behind them. But the period of rapid advances in tyre technology, the battle for tyre supremacy, had not yet broken out.

Back in Europe, a strange sense of déjà vu had enveloped the Grand Prix season, because it was a breathtaking Clark and Hill wrestling match for all but two of the victories. Those rebellious two victories went to a newcomer driving a BRM; the newcomer was Jackie Stewart, who took his BRM to victory in Italy, whilst American Richie Ginther enabled Honda to get their noses into the Grand Prix in the last race of the season in Mexico.

Clark had the edge in this, the last 1.5-litre formula season, however, despite the Lotus team's problems with the newly developed Coventry Climax 32-valve motor, and he romped home with 54 points, Graham Hill taking second place with 40 and Jackie Stewart making his presence felt in his debut season, on 33.

So while all eyes were fixed on Jim Clark for the 1966 season, with perhaps a little side bet on Jackie Stewart or Jochen Rindt, no one saw the tenacious stalwart Jack Brabham revving up behind them. The 3-litre formula had now come into effect although only Ferrari, Cooper and Brabham were set up for it. The Brabham, designed by the driver himself, was now using a Repco V8 that produced 308 bhp at 8500 rpm, which made it the least effective of the cars that year. But it was Brabham who survived the deluge in Belgium that had cars spinning like tops, caused Jackie Stewart to crash and break his collarbone and Jim Clark to abandon the race because of mechanical failure. Jack Brabham won the race as he did in Germany in another downpour when he beat off the challenges by John Surtees, now in a Cooper-Maserati after friction with Ferrari, and Jochen Rindt, winning his first German Grand Prix in superb style. In total, Brabham won four races during a season in which no car completed every single Grand Prix race. Those four victories were enough to secure the championship for him for the third time at the age of 41.

Jacky Ickx made his debut in Germany this year. Ickx would go on to gain twenty-five Formula One podium finishes.

If anyone thought Jack Brabham was going to rest on his laurels they were seriously mistaken, because he was challenging hard for the championship again the next year and was, ironically, pipped at the post by one of his own cars driven by Denny Hulme from New Zealand. Hulme claimed that year's championship with 51 points to Brabham's 46.

Jim Clark in his Lotus, 1965

Jackie Stewart relaxes with BRM teammate Graham Hill before the start of the Italian Grand Prix at Monza, 1966

And where was Jim Clark in all this? You can be sure he wasn't far away; he finished the season in third place, mainly because the new Lotus 49, although clearly a wonderful car, had teething problems.

Graham Hill had decided that if Jack still had it in him then it was time for a British "vet" to get another look in. It proved to be more than just a look in. Hill ended the 1968 season at the top of the table despite a run of bad luck, squeezing out the tenacious Jackie Stewart, who finished second. Stewart had missed several races due to injury. But as so often in motor sport, the joy of winning was dampened by tragedy. Those whom the gods love die young, and Jim Clark, who had looked set to storm through the season after winning the first F1 race of 1968, and thrill spectators for many years to come, was killed in a Formula 2 event at Hockenheim. He was thirty-two years old and had clocked up twenty-five Grand Prix victories thus beating the legendary Fangio's total.

Five drivers died that season, the last in which a track would be used without any safety modifications. As the last years of the decade approached, the times were, indeed, a changin'. Fire extinguishers became compulsory, and the cars had now begun to sprout

Jackie Stewart on his way to winning the World Championship in 1969

wings to improve the aerodynamics (although the wings were briefly banned after they took to flying off by themselves!), and the old guard of drivers were rapidly losing ground to the hungry new upstarts, one of whom now staked his claim in spectacular fashion.

Jackie Stewart had been lying in Graham Hill's slipstream for long enough, and in 1969 he accelerated to the front of the pack in his new Matra MS80. Initially, his car's fins could increase or decrease their angle according to his speed, until legislation banned adjustable wings by the time of the third race in Monaco. Stewart won the first two races, was beaten one last time by Hill in the Monaco GP, then took the next three, the Dutch, French and British, before adding the Italian in September for good measure. Stewart's domination of the season was symbolised by the Barcelona competition, where he was two laps ahead of second-placed Bruce McLaren when he crossed the finishing line, an astonishing feat only equalled in 1995. Stewart took 63 points that season. Hill's efforts to maintain his mighty run at the top were dealt a severe blow when he was injured in an accident caused by one of his tyres blowing out. It was an omen; his illustrious career was almost over.

Phil Hill, Luigi Bazzi, Carlo Chiti and Dan Gurney with Ferraris in the pits during the Portuguese Grand Prix at Monsanto, August 1959

The Dutch Grand Prix; Zandvoort. Jim Clark in his Lotus 33 winning again, July 1965

Monaco Grand Prix in Monte Carlo, 1961

X-100
MULTIGRA
16
38

Photographers stand perilously close to the track as Jochen Rindt drives his Cooper T81 Maserati in the XVIII BRDC International Trophy Race at Silverstone, 1966

Graham Hill closely followed by Jackie Stewart in their BRM P261s at the Monaco Grand Prix, May 1966

John Surtees sits in the cockpit of his stricken BRM as mechanics work on his car at the British Grand Prix in 1969. He spent only one disappointing season with the team, only finishing half of the races

The high stakes and dangers of Grand Prix racing!

TOP TO BOTTOM: Dan Gurney survives a crash at the Dutch Grand Prix after his rear brakes failed, 1960

Lorenzo Bandini of Italy crashed his Ferrari after losing control at the chicane of the Monaco Grand Prix in May 1967. The car torched the straw bales causing a fireball with the driver trapped inside. Approaching cars tried to avoid the disaster. Bandini died three days later from his horrific injuries

Observers at Hockenheim, Germany, look on in disbelief at the wreckage of the Lotus-Cosworth driven by Jim Clark. He was devastatingly killed after leaving the track and hitting a tree during a Formula Two race in 1968

Bruce McLaren getting a new set of boots on his McLaren. To his right a Ferrari driven by Chris Amon is about to shoot out of the pit lane at the French Grand Prix, 1968

Legendary DRIVERS

JUAN MANUEL FANGIO

EL MAESTRO

The Argentinean superstar who dominated the first decade of F1 and set records that will never be beaten

Juan Manuel Fangio was a man apart from his fellow racers during the early years of F1. While most competitors were young men from privileged European backgrounds, Fangio was an Argentinean mechanic. He was just about to turn 39 and had spent years honing his skills in endurance races in his home country when the British Grand Prix kicked off the FIA World Championship in 1950.

Fangio raced for Alfa Romeo in the inaugural season and topped the points going into the final Grand Prix, but car problems forced him to retire. He attempted to get back into the race by taking over a teammate's car – the rules allowed it back then – but lasted only nine more laps before technical problems struck again and Fangio retired a second time. The following year there were no such mishaps and Fangio won his first Drivers' Championship.

However, 1952 was a year to forget. New regulations banned Fangio's Alfa Romeo but he would have missed most of the season anyway after breaking his neck in a crash at a non-championship Grand Prix at Monza. It was an uncharacteristic error for a driver who rarely lost control and was known for winning races at the slowest possible speed.

A fit-again Fangio won four consecutive Drivers' Championships from 1954 to 1957. His win at the German Grand Prix was not just his final race win, it was one of the best. After a botched pit stop left him a minute behind the leaders, Fangio set fastest lap after fastest lap to win. The greatest driver of his era, who won nearly half of the Grand Prix he started, had left his best performance for the end.

» **Juan Manuel Fangio corners in his Ferrari on his way to another victory at the The Syracuse Grand Prix, 1956**

Fangio has the highest win percentage of any F1 driver, having taken victory in 47% of the races he started

Legendary **DRIVERS**

ALBERTO ASCARI

HIS FATHER'S SON

The first double world champion whose death was an eerie echo of his father's

Ascari was on course to win Lancia's first Grand Prix before he crashed at Monaco; four days later he was dead

Leading from start to finish, Alberto Ascari after completing his victory at the Dutch Grand Prix in 1952

Young Alberto Ascari was the biggest fan of his father – racing star Antonio who won four pre-World Championship Grand Prix in the 1920s – so it hit hard when he died in a crash at the 1925 French Grand Prix. But he didn't avoid the sport that killed his dad – Ascari was determined to follow in his footsteps. He was recruited by Enzo Ferrari in time for the first FIA World Championship in 1950.

He picked up his first race wins in 1951 before storming to victory in the 1952 Drivers' Championship by winning the last six races of the season. No driver could get past Ascari and his lucky blue helmet. He held the lead for 304 consecutive laps across five races, a record that will surely never be broken. Ascari was almost as dominant in 1953, winning five races to become the first multiple world champion, before accepting an offer to drive for Lancia. Ascari was open about his motivations – it was all about the money – but he missed almost all of 1954 while his new team prepared the cars.

There was the potential for a long and successful partnership – Ascari earned pole position and set the fastest lap in Lancia's debut Grand Prix – but things went wrong at the 1955 Monaco Grand Prix. Ascari lost control while leading the race and his car flew through the fence and into Monte Carlo harbour. The Lancia sank; Ascari bobbed to the surface.

Four days later, a largely uninjured Ascari attended a Ferrari test session at Monza. He asked to drive but the car skidded and flipped after three laps. Ascari was flung from his seat and suffered fatal injuries. Were there portents of his death? His father died on 26 July 1925; Alberto died on 26 May 1955. Both were 36 and had won 13 Grand Prix. Both had survived crashes four days before their life-ending accidents at seemingly innocuous left turns.

Legendary DRIVERS

JACK BRABHAM

AUSSIE KNIGHT

Forceful on the track but unassuming off it, Braham dominated the second decade of F1 action

Only the second Australian ever to race in Formula One, Sir John Arthur 'Jack' Brabham became the first Antipodean to be crowned champion in 1959, winning the coveted title three times across a glittering Grand Prix career which spanned 17 seasons and three decades. He had volunteered to be a pilot with the Royal Australian Air Force in the Second World War but ultimately served as a mechanic, satisfying his craving for speed later in life on four wheels rather than in the skies.

He made his F1 debut at the age of 29 with the Cooper team in the 1955 British Grand Prix, but was forced to retire on debut due to engine failure. In his first four years he featured in 15 Grands Prix, his best finish fourth in Monaco in 1958, but the following season Brabham's aggressive style combined with his finely tuned

Jack Brabham in his Brabham-Repco BT19 at the Italian Grand Prix, Monza 1966

understanding of both the mechanic capabilities and limitations of the cars he drove finally paid dividends.

A season-opening and maiden F1 win in Monaco in May set the tone. He also triumphed at the British Grand Prix at Aintree, outpacing runner-up Stirling Moss, but Brabham and his Cooper-Climax were only one of three entrants who could still claim the world title going into the year's final race at the USA Grand Prix in Florida in December. The Australian was only fourth after the 42 laps on the Sebring International Raceway but it was a result that secured him the F1 crown for the first time.

Five consecutive victories in the Netherlands, Belgium, France, the UK and Portugal saw him comfortably retain his title in 1960 ahead of Kiwi Bruce McLaren. By 1966 he had parted ways with Cooper and founded his eponymous Brabham F1 team and in a year in which the fabled British quartet of John Surtees, Graham Hill, Jim Clark and Jackie Stewart all lined up on the grid, the Australian won four of the nine races to seal a hat-trick of crowns. His title triumph remains the only time in the sport's history a driver secured the championship in a car bearing his own name.

His farewell F1 season came in 1970. Brabham was knighted in recognition for his services to motorsport eight years later and died in Queensland in 2014 at the age of 88.

Brabham (#16) overcoming his nearest rivals at the Dutch Grand Prix, 1966

Legendary DRIVERS

GRAHAM HILL

MR MONACO

The two-time world champion and the only driver to have won the Triple Crown of Motorsport

Graham Hill didn't exactly set the world alight on his debut in Formula 1. Racing for Lotus during its first F1 campaign, Hill's first seven races ended in retirement. His two seasons with Colin Chapman saw Hill fail to win a single point, though he would return later in his career with more success.

In the meantime Hill switched to BRM, an outfit that seemed to have as poor an outlook as Lotus, but Hill put in long hours with his mechanics to help improve the cars until, in 1962, he won four races and topped the Drivers' Championship. Over the next three years he finished second, twice to Jim Clark and once to John Surtees. The loss to Surtees in 1964 was particularly hard. Hill scored 41 points to Surtees' 40, but since a driver's best six finishes only counted, Hill's total dropped to 39 while Surtees – who retired four times – stayed on 40.

Hill returned to Lotus in 1967 and teamed up with

Hill drove a Lotus in the team's inaugural Grand Prix in the principality and returned to triumph in Monte Carlo five times

Jim Clark, but the two-time world champion was killed after one Grand Prix in 1968. Hill responded by driving the fragile and unpredictable Lotus without fear, winning three races and finishing second in three more to match his late teammate by winning a second Drivers' Championship.

Hill's time as a frontrunner came to an end a year later. When his Lotus stalled at the US Grand Prix, he got out to push-start his own car. He got going again but a tyre failure sent the car into a bank and Hill, who had not buckled his safety belt, was thrown from the car. Although he recovered from serious leg injuries and returned to F1, his six years with Walker, Brabham and his own Hill team were as unsuccessful as his first two years in the sport. His death in 1975 robbed him of the chance to see his son Damon become the first son of a world champion to also win the title.

Graham Hill overseeing in the driving seat his young protégé son Damon at Silverstone, 1967

Legendary
DRIVERS

JIM CLARK
MR SMOOTH

The double world champion who triumphed in one of the most dominant seasons in F1 history

The Lotus 25 that helped Clark win the 1963 championship was stronger yet lighter than the previous models and proved dominant on the track

The danger inherent in being a Formula 1 driver was made clear to Jim Clark in only his second race. Chris Bristow and Alan Stacey were killed in separate crashes within a few minutes and a few hundred metres of each other, yet the race continued and Clark finished fifth to pick up his first Grand Prix points. Only after the race was complete were flecks of Bristow's blood spotted on Clark's car.

The following year, Clark touched wheels with the Ferrari of Wolfgang von Trips. The German's car slid up an embankment and into a fence, killing him as well as 15 spectators.

Clark held his nerve after these early tragedies to become one of the top drivers of the 1960s. He won the Drivers' Championship twice, in 1963 and 1965, on both occasions achieving the maximum score of 54 at a time when only a driver's top six scores from the ten-race season were counted. An oil leak on the last few laps of the last Grand Prix of 1964 robbed him of the opportunity to add to his titles. It was his maiden triumph in 1963 for which Clark will always be remembered, though. He won seven of ten races and only finished off the podium on one occasion. He lapped every competitor at the Dutch Grand Prix and finished the Belgian Grand Prix almost five minutes ahead of his nearest rival, despite suffering gearbox issues that meant he had to hold the lever in place when fifth gear was selected. Clark and his Lotus were simply unstoppable.

Clark was still a contender in 1968 and won the first race of the season before heading to the Hockenheimring to compete for Lotus in a Formula 2 race. Clark's car left the track after five laps – a deflating rear tyre the likely cause – and he suffered fractures to his neck and skull, dying of his injuries on the way to the hospital. At a time when fatalities were sadly common, the loss of a double world champion still shocked the motorsport world.

Clark relaxing before a race in 1965. As well as Formula 1, Clark also competed in sports cars, touring cars and the Indy 500

TOP TO MIDDLE: Jim was given a chance by Colin Chapman (behind Clark) after he came second to his future Lotus team boss in a race

Clark in the Lotus 49 Ford Cosworth at the Mexican Grand Prix, 1967

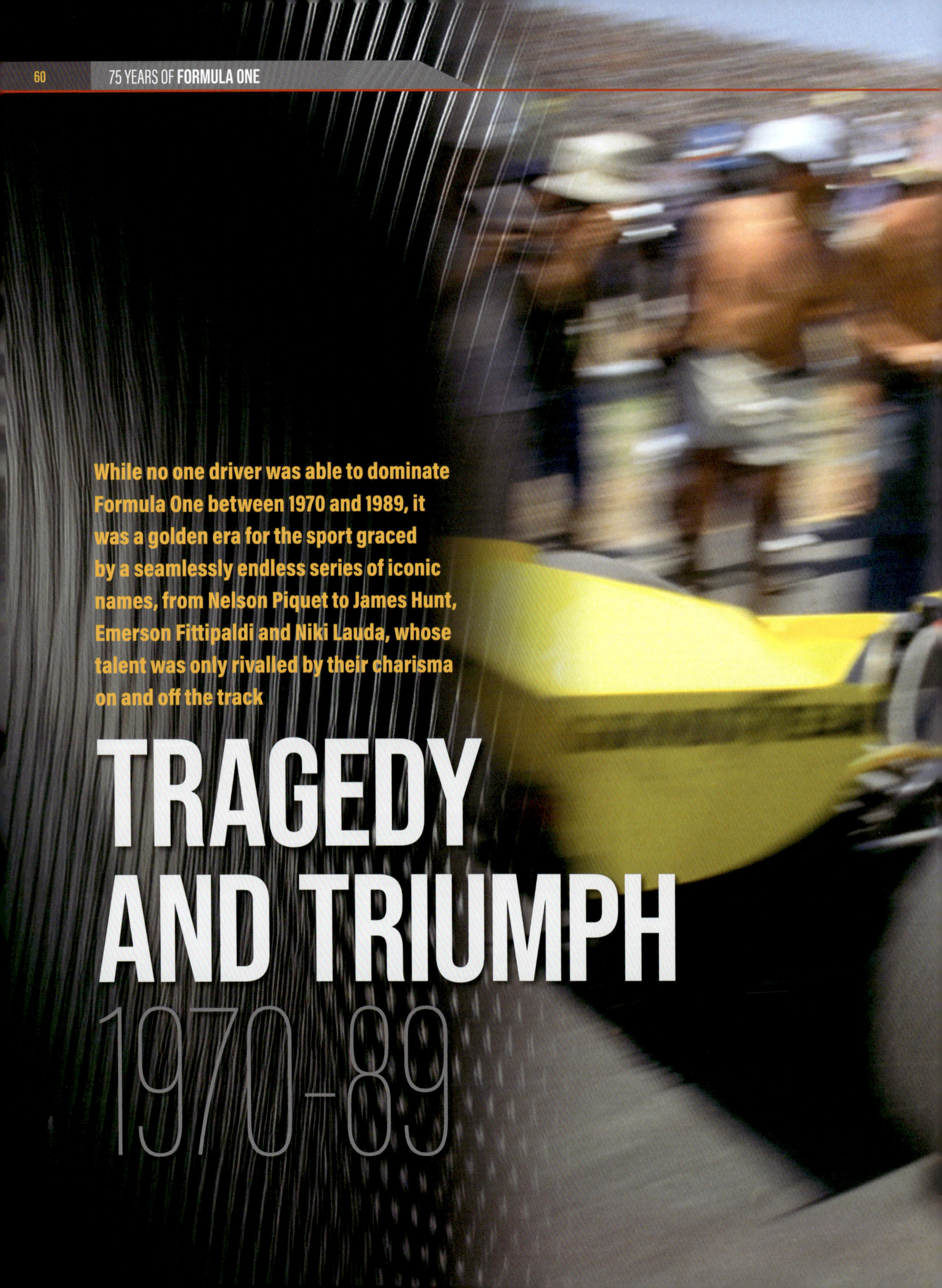

While no one driver was able to dominate Formula One between 1970 and 1989, it was a golden era for the sport graced by a seamlessly endless series of iconic names, from Nelson Piquet to James Hunt, Emerson Fittipaldi and Niki Lauda, whose talent was only rivalled by their charisma on and off the track

TRAGEDY AND TRIUMPH 1970-89

Emerson Fittipaldi blasts out of the pits driving a Copersucar-Fittipaldi F5A at the Brazilian Grand Prix, 1978

What is there to say about the extraordinary season of racing that began a bright new decade? The new young hopefuls were out in force; the Scot Jackie Stewart, driving a March 701 owned by Ken Tyrrell, Brazilian Emerson Fittipaldi in a Lotus-Ford, Austrian Jochen Rindt in the new Lotus-Ford 72, and Jackie Ickx in his Ferrari. It was going to be a cut-throat season. The new Brabham-Ford BT 33 was unveiled, with Jack now in his twenty-third year behind the wheel. The indefatigable Mr. Brabham even took victory in the season's initial Grand Prix in South Africa. It was the Australian's last race win.

There was a warning at the Spanish Grand Prix of what was to come, when Jackie Oliver and Jackie Ickx's cars both caught fire. The drivers escaped. And then Bruce McLaren was killed whilst testing a Can-Am car at the Goodwood circuit in southern England. But the show always had to go on, and Jochen Rindt suddenly burst into action showing why he was going to be the man to beat in the future, when he won five Grands Prix in six races. Rindt and Ickx had locked horns for the championship and carried the battle through onto the German course on August 2. A battle that Rindt won. The struggle for the championship was intense between the two rivals especially when Ickx took the next victory in Austria. Everything was shaping up for a classic showdown at Monza. And then this unforgiving sport ended another brilliant driver's life; Rindt suffered a brake system failure, causing his car to speed into and under a crash barrier during a practice run. He did not survive. At 28, the Grand Prix had claimed another of her heroes.

In deference to the young man's talent and sacrifice,

Belgian driver Jacky Ickx stood beside his Ferrari before the start of the French Grand Prix, 1971

Jochen Rindt after winning the Dutch Grand Prix in 1970, alongside Lotus team owner Colin Chapman

Another win and celebration for Jackie Stewart

Jochen Rindt was awarded the championship title posthumously. He was the only driver ever to be honoured in this way.

The scintillating four years that followed could best be described as the Stewart-Fittipaldi spectacular, although in 1971, Jackie Stewart took his second World Championship, his Tyrrell searing the race courses as he dominated the entire season, finishing on 62 points, far ahead of second-placed Ronnie Peterson on 33. Fittipaldi had to be content with sixth place. But he would have revenge in 1972. And how!

In the year in which the Brabham team was taken over by Bernie Ecclestone, a wealthy London businessman, Emerson Fittipaldi suddenly proved that he was a class act in his redeveloped Lotus-Ford 72D, winning five of the Grands Prix (Spain was only his second F1 victory, that is a measure of how his career had skyrocketed), although Jackie Stewart, who won four victories, fought him tooth and nail all the way.

Emerson Fittipaldi in his Lotus-Ford and crew preparing for the Swedish Grand Prix in June 1973

Stewart lost out to Fittipaldi at the British Grand Prix, coming in four seconds behind his rival after a high-octane jousting match at Brands Hatch. Fittipaldi took the crown in fine style with 61 points to Jackie Stewart's 45, becoming the youngest championship winner ever at the age of 25 years and 273 days.

The wet track at Monaco had shown that the super-wide tyres of the modern racing cars could not cope well with water, sending cars spinning almost on every lap. Some of the Surtees TS9 rims were eighteen inches wide, and the Lotus 72D had 14 inch tyres on the front and 9 inch tyres at the rear. Many of the cars that year had a great deal of the weight positioned over the rear axle, with wings mounted behind it. And this year saw the introduction of laterally drilled disc brakes, which were more effective at dissipating heat.

With Fittipaldi taking the first two victories of the New Year, Stewart had a fight on his hands; but the Tyrrell team needn't have worried, for in the season that saw the young James Hunt pick up 14 points, and the first appearance of a safety car, Jackie Stewart tucked five victories under his belt and 71 points, to win the championship for the third time. But his victory was shrouded in a familiar sadness, because Stewart's teammate François Cevert had been killed during practice for the US Grand Prix. Stewart was so distressed over his friend's death that after twenty-seven victories, he ended his career there and then, never racing again.

With Stewart no longer a rival, Fittipaldi might have been expected to have had everything his own way from then on. Not so, because not only was James Hunt chomping at the bit, Niki Lauda had arrived driving a Ferrari 312B3, in which he took pole position nine times in fifteen starts. This boy meant business. Initially, his lack of experience showed, however, and the title eventually did go to Fittipaldi, who had changed to the McLaren team for the 1974 season.

Although Fittipaldi came second the following season, no one could have foreseen that he had won his last World Championship. In fact, no one could

Ronnie Peterson in his Lotus leading the field at the Dutch Grand Prix 1973 ahead of Jackie Stewart in his Tyrrell, Carlos Pace's Surtees Fina-Ford and François Cevert's Tyrrell

have foreseen the events of that season. It was the year Niki Lauda fulfilled his potential in brilliant style, his "unbelievable year" as he put it, in a Ferrari; the Ferrari 1312T, to be precise, a car that wiped the floor with its competitors, although it was not until the fifth Grand Prix in Monaco that car and driver gelled into a fearsome winning combination. As the season got under way, Fittipaldi continued where he had left off and won the first race. Lauda's Ferrari was nowhere, even though he had taken pole in Barcelona where the Italian Lella Lombardi gained the first women's point, coming in sixth.

And then, all of a sudden, the Ferrari was everywhere. Lauda took another eight pole positions and five victories. James Hunt managed to beat him to second position in Holland. Jochen Mass popped into the table on seventh place that year in his McLaren, as Lauda whipped his Ferrari around the course to take 64.5 points, seeing off Fittipaldi in second place on 45. It had been an astonishing year for the Austrian. The duel with Hunt proved prophetic, because these would be the two drivers to watch in the 1976 season.

The thrill of the 1975 season had only just ebbed away when driving legend Graham Hill crashed his Piper Aztec light plane. It was one crash too many, and one that he did not walk away from. One of Britain's legendary drivers was gone.

Lauda and Hunt delivered one of the most dramatic years of racing ever seen, in 1976. Lauda staked his claim

Niki Lauda leading and going on to win the Monaco Grand Prix, 1975

early on with two emphatic wins and a second place in the US race. Hunt started his pursuit in Spain, where he was initially disqualified after he had overtaken Lauda halfway through and taken the victory. The offence? Apparently his car had been too wide; his points were only reinstated many months later. Hunt, who had eight pole positions that year, was disqualified on another occasion for driving illegally; i.e., swapping cars following a restart of the race during the British Grand Prix. Nothing could stop Lauda from gaining his second consecutive title, it seemed. Going into the German Grand Prix he had won five races to Hunt's two. That German Grand Prix will go down in history for the wrong reasons. On the second lap, Lauda's car started to spin. It hit the embankment and burst into flames and the Ferrari was then struck by two more cars. Trapped inside, Lauda inhaled toxic gases from which he went into a coma lasting for several days, and many feared he would not survive. His burns were appalling. With Lauda hospitalised, Hunt used the opportunity well and won four races. It was astounding that Lauda was back behind the wheel after just five weeks, determined to take the title; but he had really come back too soon, and he couldn't prevent Hunt from winning the championship with 69 points, just one ahead of Lauda.

The charismatic James Hunt being interviewed in the Silverstone pit lane, 1976

Lauda and Hunt, friendly rivalry on and off track

One last note on the season; Jacky Ickx crashed in the US race and was fortunate to come out alive; after that he never seemed to recover his old form and enthusiasm, and left F1 for good in 1979.

Niki Lauda was still too good a driver to be denied for long, and with consistently strong performances in 1977, he took the World Championship for a second time, with 72 points. Hunt only managed fifth place, even though he had won three races compared to Lauda's two. But he had been forced to retire from eight races. The vagaries of the sport, however, meant that Lauda would not win the championship again until 1984.

Renault had now returned to the fold after an absence of seventy years, with a turbo-charged car. It may not have been too steady on its tyres, so to speak, but it was pointing towards the future of car technology.

The number of Grands Prix in a season had now expanded considerably; there were sixteen races in 1978, and the stresses on car and driver were immense. Niki Lauda had changed to Brabham this year after friction at Ferrari, but this was to be the glory year for America.

Italian-American Mario Andretti had already made his presence felt for the previous two seasons in his Lotus, coming home sixth and third. Now he was to make that last leap to the top in his Lotus 79, which enhanced the so-called ground effect, whereby the underside of the car was shaped so as to generate as much downforce and as little drag as possible. Andretti took the first race in Argentina, and having been victorious in six races, won the championship with 64 points. The pinnacle achievement of a ten-year dream. No other American has won the championship since. His team, Lotus, took the constructor's title. Andretti was not completely spared the merciless sacrifices of the sport; his teammate, Ronnie Peterson, twice runner-up in the championship, the fastest man of his time, crashed his car at Monza. Hunt and two other drivers released him from the blaze, but the Swedish driver died later in hospital.

There were changes aplenty between 1979 and 1983; even the championship would change hands every year with a new name appearing at the top of the table each time.

Mario Andretti navigating Druids at the British Grand Prix, Brands Hatch in 1978

Perhaps it was something to do with the impending ringing in of the new decade, but Lauda walked out on Brabham, and the glamorous, tousled James Hunt called it a day for his racing career. Australian Alan Jones raced himself back into the table for that last year of the 70's, and for Jody Scheckter, who been in the top ten ever since 1974, coming second in 1977, it was time to stand in the spotlight. Scheckter, despite an accident in Argentina, improved as the season progressed, driving with more focus and consistency. His teammate at Ferrari, Canadian Gilles Villeneuve, father of the future champion Jacques, who had entered the top ten the previous year, would come second this year, his highest ever placing. Villeneuve was just four points adrift, but had followed team instructions to allow Scheckter the title. It was just as well, for South African Scheckter abandoned F1 in 1980 and Ferrari plunged into the not-quite-good-enough abyss until the year 2000, when Michael Schumacher finally gave them another victory.

With the start of the 80s, came new faces to shuffle up the pack; and what skills and thrills the newcomers brought with them. The Brazilian Nelson Piquet climbed behind the Brabham wheel, and a talented young Alain Prost joined McLaren, although he would have to wait until the following season for his star to rise like Piquet's. But the star of the year 1980 was to be the Australian

Jody Scheckter leads the 1978 British Grand Prix in his Wolf before retiring. On his tail were Alan Jones's Williams, Niki Lauda's Brabham and Riccardo Patrese in his Arrows

Alan Jones driving a Williams FW07 at first, and then the magnificent FW07B.

Skirted wings on cars were producing a downforce that enabled cornering speeds to rise alarmingly, and a driver could take three seconds from his lap speed of the previous year. The wheels now took corners as though they were on rails, which produced enormous tension in the outward-straining bodies of the drivers. The carbon fibre chassis, which reduced the possibility of chassis twist, had been introduced by Brabham the year before and would soon become standard on all cars; and the computer made its appearance when Tyrrell used one to monitor a new suspension system. It didn't help to produce any noticeable improvements in performance, however.

Alan Jones was given the fight of his life by Nelson Piquet, and with just two drives left before the end of the season, Nelson Piquet was one point ahead of the Williams driver; both men had three victories apiece. At Montréal, Jones forced his rival into the crash barriers and there was an enormous collision that led to the race being stopped. When it restarted, Piquet, in his spare car, had to withdraw when his engine failed, leaving Jones to take victory. There was bad luck for Piquet in the final Grand Prix in the United States, too, when he had to withdraw after 25 laps. Jones won the race and the championship.

Alain Prost's Renault is hotly pursued by a chasing Alan Jones in his Williams, 1981

Nelson Piquet in the Parmalat Brabham at the British Grand Prix, Brands Hatch in 1982

Piquet's season came in 1981; he squeezed home by one point in front of the Argentinean Carlos Reutemann with whom he had fought a tyre to tyre race in a year that saw Alain Prost in his Renault rise threateningly to number five in the final table. After claiming his first victory in Dijon, Prost followed it with two more. The most exciting race of the season, however, involved Villeneuve, Jacques Laffite, John Watson, Elio de Angelis and Reutemann in Spain. In this five-man tussle, Villeneuve proved that he still had the nerve of a Formula One champion and took the race.

With Ferrari, Ligier-Matra and Renault in the running this year and taking seven victories, the British manufacturers no longer had it all their own way. A new method had been found to counter the loss of downforce due to the removal of the skirts; hydraulic units were developed to lower the chassis as the car was in motion, so that standing still, the minimum required height of 60mm from the ground could be achieved. Gordon Murray, the Brabham designer, first introduced this innovation, which brought ground clearance to almost zero when the car was in motion. Unfortunately, the type of chassis required to cope with this was so rigid that driving a Formula One car had become a bone-shaking experience endangering the drivers' health.

Alain Prost began to climb the table inexorably, and it was just a matter of time before he tasted glory with a championship victory. But 1982 was to be a Williams' year again, this time with Keke Rosberg taking the winning chequered flag. This year was not without its difficulties, although it did see Niki Lauda re-enter the competition and the top ten table for the first time since 1978. Like a struck match, Rosberg flared once, before

Keke Rosberg in his Williams at the Italian Grand Prix, 1982

Gillles Villenueve lost in thought, sat on his Ferrari

his career then died away. In a season when many drivers had claimed victories, he only won one race; the last time this had happened was in 1958 when Mike Hawthorn had pulled off the same trick to claim the title.

Difficulties had arisen off the circuit in rule disputes between two competing organizations, the Formula One Constructors Association (FOCA) and FISA, which had been stewing since 1979. There was a drivers' strike led by Niki Lauda against the so-called super licenses that Lauda felt would restrict a driver's freedom to change teams. There were disputes, too, over water-cooled brakes and when Ferrari used two rear wings, and there was a boycott of a FOCA team for the San Marino race. This all paled into insignificance when Gilles Villenueve was killed in the qualifying rounds of the Belgian Grand Prix after Jochen Mass had moved aside to let the Canadian pass only to find himself right in his path. The collision hurled Villeneuve out of his car and he died later that evening. Lotus boss Colin Chapman also died that year from a heart attack, and both Alan Jones and Carlos Reutemann decided to call it a day.

While Alain Prost went from strength to strength, there was a new kid on the grid in Formula Ford 2000. It would be a while before he made his presence felt, but Damon Hill would soon show the world that he had inherited his father's speed genes.

In 1983, Prost went head-to-head with Piquet for the championship in a contest that went right down to the wire in the last Grand Prix of the season in South Africa. At that point, Alain Prost was leading the championship with 57 points, and Nelson Piquet was just behind him with 55. Prost was fifth on the grid but fought his way up to third place before he was defeated by a turbo failure. Piquet took his second championship. He was the first driver to do so in a turbo-driven car, of which more had appeared that year; Alfa Romeo's V8 1497cc unit, and Honda's V6 engine could be seen at the Geneva Motor Show. These turbo engines were now developing between 700 and 800bhp in cars that the Formula One rules now dictated had to weigh at least 540 kg. But the turbo would not kick in for between half a second and one second after pressure was applied to the pedal, a delay that could cause a car to slide when exiting a corner. Other new rules stated that the rear wings must be set at the maximum height of 100cm, although the width was restricted to 100cm, which reduced the downforce somewhat. But more rear wings with vertical side plates appeared this year, too, and these new wing designs helped to increase the downforce again. And the lightning fuel and tyre stops that Brabham had tried out the previous year had been so successful that all the other teams now did the same thing.

Nigel Mansell at the British Grand Prix 1983, in the Lotus 94T

British driver Nigel Mansell had driven his Formula One debut in 1980 but had failed to make the top ten table; now, in 1984, he finally made it, and would not leave it until he retired in 1992, driving his Lotus 95T to a number nine place. On equal points, 13, was another new face in the table destined to become a legend, Ayrton Senna.

Prost was now a McLaren driver for 1984

But the action at the top in 1984 was between Niki Lauda and Alain Prost and only a hair's breadth separated the two drivers – who were now teammates, both driving McLarens. With refuelling now banned (it would be made legal again in 1994), and turbocharged engines allowed to use just 220 litres of fuel per race instead of 250 (this 'handicap' was countered by chilling the fuel, which 'shrank' it, sometimes to below -50 degrees, and that meant that some 15 litres of additional fuel could be squeezed into the tank), all was set for a classic contest.

And it truly was a battle of the Olympians. Lauda and Prost; the two unyielding rivals jousted for victory over the last seven races giving no one else a chance. Prost won seven victories to Lauda's five. The championship came down to the competition in Portugal with Lauda ahead on points. The deciding race was as dramatic as anyone could have wished for; it all hung on just one half point. Lauda only needed a second place to secure the championship, but he was having trouble passing Nigel Mansell, until eighteen laps before the end. For Lauda, this could possibly have been the last bite of the cherry, which, indeed, it proved to be, as he came in

Niki Lauda on the charge at the Dallas Grand Prix USA, 1984

tenth the following year before taking off his Grand Prix helmet for the last time. Prost grabbed the lead from Keke Rosberg in the Honda-Williams and held it through to the finish. But the final decision had lain with Nigel Mansell, because when he had spun out of control on the eighteenth lap, he had handed Lauda second place and, therefore, the championship.

Even though Ayrton Senna came home in joint ninth place with Nigel Mansell at the end of the season, both with just 13 points, he had gained his first honours amongst the big boys, and it was clear that here was a major new talent. Mansell had just squeaked onto the table by pushing his car over the line during the Monaco Grand Prix, and fainting as a result.

Over the course of the next three seasons, Senna began to put the notches in his exhaust pipe. The McLaren, too, driven by both Prost and Lauda in its TAG-Porsche engine version with twelve victories in sixteen championship races and later to become Senna's car of choice, was also going to prove hard to beat. It dominated the tables until Michael Schumacher came along in the early 1990s. The McLarens had been using Michelin tyres and they, together with all the other teams that had been using Michelin rubber, received a shock when the French firm said that it would no longer take part in Grand Prix racing.

On the track, following two years as runner up, the brief but exciting Alain Prost era had begun. The 1985 season, in fact, turned out to be one of the most nerve-wrenching there has ever been, according to ardent aficionados of the sport. Prost was made to fight for the title by the Italian Michele Alboreto in his Ferrari, who had soon racked up forty-six points from seven podium appearances. So Ferrari were looking like champions; at least until the Austrian Grand Prix. It was here, that Niki Lauda announced his retirement, and here that Alain Prost began his inspiring fight back.

Prost was on pole position, his average speed 155 mph. McLaren was king on the Österreichring – pardon the poetic lapse, but this was a year for poetry – in Austria, an extremely fast and scenic track. Lauda was unlucky when turbo failure forced his exit and Prost took the chequered flag first.

Stefan Bellof, a rising star of Formula One, was another of the many drivers who did not live long enough to fulfill their potential and died when they were off the Grand Prix track; Bellof was killed during the World Endurance Championships. The Dutch Grand Prix was the last one Bellof drove, and it was also the thirty-fourth and last to be held in the Netherlands; here, too, Niki Lauda drove his last winning race before he retired.

Despite Nigel Mansell putting in a great showing and winning at Brands Hatch, his first home victory, and in South Africa, it was Prost who put in the most victories,

Star in the making – a young Ayrton Senna driving for Toleman, 1984

Michele Alboreto's Ferrari in the pits at the German Grand Prix Nürburgring, 1985

taking five by the end of the season in his McLaren MP 4/2B. And Prost took the coveted World Championship with 73 points, ahead of Alboreto on 53.

He repeated the trick the following year, chased all the way, this time by Nigel Mansell in his Williams, who was just two points behind him at the end of the season with 70. The talented Nigel Mansell would come runner-up three times before he was allowed to taste the sweetness of a championship winner's podium appearance. In 1986, everything had come down to the final race in Australia with Mansell favourite to win. But it was destined not to be; heartbreakingly for the British driver and his fans, Mansell's tyre blew out on the sixty-third lap.

Mansell's rival the following year would be his own teammate. Nelson Piquet had never quite gone away since his last victory in 1983. Having changed over to the Williams team in 1986, he was suddenly given a new lease of life and throttled his way back to the top in 1987. That year saw four drivers battle it out for top place; Prost, Senna, Piquet and Mansell. Mansell once again encountered bad luck; two retirements at Monaco and Detroit left him trailing, and when he crashed during qualifying and hurt his back, which put him out of the race at Suzuka in Japan, it ultimately cost him the championship, despite six victory podiums. Prost and the McLaren eventually wilted and finished the season fourth behind Senna with 57 points on third.

Senna was seemingly fearless and consequently took risks with his driving, which was absolutely breathtaking to watch but left many people wondering if the young Brazilian would always be able to escape an accident by a hair's breadth. This championship, however, was firmly

Nigel Mansell driving his Williams at the 1985 European Grand Prix, Brands Hatch

Prost takes the chequered flag and the 1986 World Championship in Adelaide with McLaren

in the hands of Nelson Piquet, whose consistency had brought rich rewards, and he won the title with two races still to go. And the rich rewards that motor racing could now bring, with television interest so high, meant that the top ten teams in each season would now be able to travel to the Grand Prix the following year free of charge.

Another Austrian, Gerhard Berger, had entered the top ten for the first time in 1986 and would stay around for many years challenging all those around him on the track, though he would never equal his countryman Lauda's record. In 1988, he was to rise to number three in a Ferrari, a position he would gain for a second time in 1990, although in a McLaren at that point, sharing the position with Nelson Piquet, another irrepressible driver. Berger chose the wrong year to peak, however, because Ayrton Senna was also on top form.

Turbocharged engines were making their final appearances this year of 1988, and would give way to the naturally aspirated engines in 1989. And Benetton began to taste success when their car, with a Ford DFR 3.5 V8 engine and driven by Belgian Thierry Boutsen, came in fourth.

It was an extraordinary season; the table shows that two men won every race except one, with Gerhard Berger snatching a victory at Monza in Italy. It is, perhaps, not surprising to learn that the two men were those titans of the track, Ayrton Senna and Alain Prost. These two extraordinary drivers would lock horns for the next four heart-pounding seasons. In 1988, that meant, that the year was practically a whitewash for McLaren-Honda, because Senna and Prost were now teammates. And when the season was over there were just three points separating them.

It was unfortunate for Prost that Senna was on unbeatable form and took home the greatest number of points ever in a Grand Prix season; 90. And the race that perhaps symbolised the Brazilian's extraordinary fierce determination was the deciding contest at Suzuka in Japan. A win here would guarantee Senna the title, but he began the race in fourteenth position because his car stalled, and it was only because of the sloping track at the start that he was able to stay in the race at all. It was an inspired piece of driving by the Brazilian, because by lap 27, he was in the lead. Not only did he stay there and take the race and the championship, he also drove three consecutive fastest laps and set a new lap record. He won eight of that season's races; Prost won seven. Had it not been for the rule that dictated that only the eleven highest scores counted, (no, best not to even think about it!) Prost would have won, having scored eleven points more. In 1964, Graham Hill lost the championship for the same reason, and the system was only changed in 1991.

All in all, then, a season to savour.

So what would happen the following year? Would the rivalry that had been sharpened by Prost's open criticism of Senna's driving now cause problems? Was Senna unreachable?

1989. The 3.5-litre atmospheric engines proved as fast as the 1.5-litre turbo engines, a fact which bemused everyone slightly. Gone was the turbo-lag effect, acceleration was admirable, 124.2 mph (200km/h) from a standing start in

Prost and Senna. Good manners of being McLaren teammates soon eroded into a fierce battle of the titans rivalry

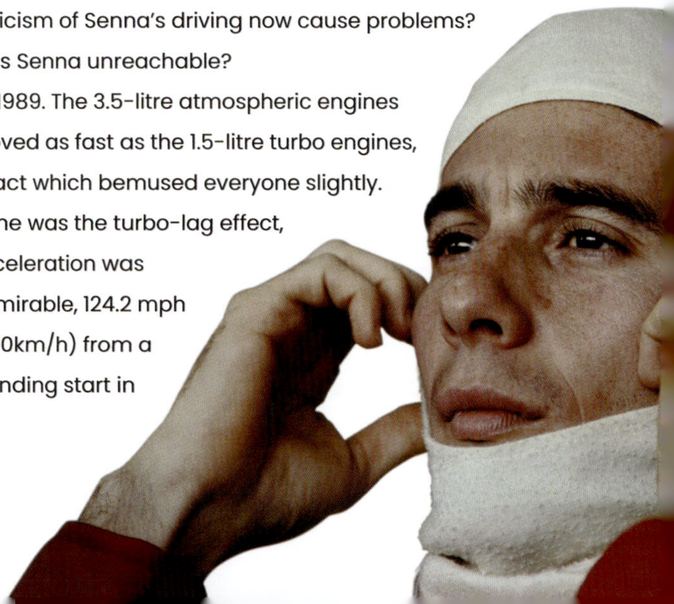

5.2 or 5.3 seconds, and corners could be assailed more easily. Using the so-called "Concorde beak", which was narrow and allowed for wider front wings, also became the norm for many designers. What was not to like? Nigel Mansell had driven some superb races the previous year and had now changed to Ferrari, where his skill was proving to be a threatening red devil to McLaren, although Italian Riccardo Patrese in a Williams beat him down to fourth spot that year.

All eyes were, of course, once more riveted upon Senna and Prost; the latter was to win thirteen pole positions (he equalled Jim Clark's thirty-three that year), and the tensions between the two surged. Prost felt that Senna's driving was reckless and, therefore, dangerous, and they began arguing off track at Imola, Prost claiming that Senna had breached a team ethics code not to challenge the car leading at the first corner. Prost also felt aggrieved at his team, sensing that he was being disadvantaged, and announced that he would drive for Ferrari the following season. With two retirements in France and Britain, and being driven into by Nigel Mansell on lap 48 at Estoril, Senna was on the back foot. At Suzuka, Prost must have wondered if either he or Senna would survive the battles, when the Brazilian's aggressive behaviour sent them both spinning. Having announced he was leaving McLaren, it was ironic that the winner that year was Alain Prost, by a decisive margin from Senna; 81 points to 60, Prost's third title and very well deserved.

Season footnote; Nigel Mansell overtook and beat Senna at Hockenheim, nearly thirty seconds clear at the flag, in what was one of the most brilliant races of his life.

Ayrton Senna deep in thought as he prepares to race

Big in Japan. After a poor grid start, Senna puts on an incredible display of sheer grit to win the Japanese Grand Prix at Suzuka, beating Prost to the title in 1988

Jochen Rindt in the pits with his wife Nina during a practice session, Italian Grand Prix 1970

Rindt takes Mirabeau corner near the five-star Hotel Metropole Monte Carlo at the Monaco Grand Prix in 1970

Jacky Ickx sprints in his Ferrari 312B during the Monaco Grand Prix, 1970

Jackie Stewart with a relaxed look on the grid of the 1971 Monaco Grand Prix, sitting on the wheel of his Tyrrell 003

26
26

Clutching a clipboard, Lotus team principal Colin Chapman oversees mechanics of Ronnie Peterson's car at the German Grand Prix, 1975

James Hunt in his title winning year, 1976

Ferrari's polesetter Niki Lauda with his car in the pit lane ahead of the Spanish Grand Prix, Montjuïc circuit 1975

Marlboro
TEXACO

Gilles Villeneuve gestures for adjustments to be made on his Ferrari at the Austrian Grand Prix, Spielberg 1979

Brabham team boss Bernie Ecclestone (left) and designer Gordon Murray discuss Nelson Piquet's car in the pits, Austrian Grand Prix, Spielberg 1981

Ayrton Senna blasts his McLaren MP4/4 through the streets of the Monaco Grand Prix, 1988

Legendary **DRIVERS**

JACKIE STEWART

THE FLYING SCOT

Jackie Stewart was not only a great champion, he helped usher in a new era of safety consciousness

Many men have achieved immortality through their exploits on a racing circuit, but only a select few have influenced the sport of Formula 1 to the extent that they have actually saved lives. Ayrton Senna's fatal crash at Imola in 1994 turned out to be a heroic sacrifice as it forced the sport to instigate a raft of changes to improve safety. However, it shouldn't be forgotten that Jackie Stewart had laid the foundation for those changes decades earlier. In fact, before Stewart came along, it is not unreasonable to argue that there were no safety standards in Formula 1 at all.

Driving was not the first love of John Young Stewart – that position is held by shooting, at which he excelled, being nearly good enough to represent Great Britain at the Olympics. Once he got behind the wheel of a car, however, there was almost literally no stopping him – he

Jackie on the winners podium of the French Grand Prix, Paul Ricard Circuit 1971

caught the eye of Ken Tyrrell and raced in British Formula 3 in 1963, displaying such dominance that he once won seven consecutive races.

FORMULA 1

Stewart's Formula 1 career began with BRM in 1965, alongside Graham Hill. The season comprised just ten races at the time, with only the six best results counting, and Stewart finished third in the Drivers' Championship despite only managing a single race victory, at the Italian Grand Prix. He won the first race of the following season, but only managed to complete two more races in a disappointing year that saw him finish in seventh place. It was a similar story in 1967, as he failed to finish in nine of the 11 races.

Stewart was on a personal crusade to make the sport safer. At Belgium, in 1966, he had found himself stuck in a ditch with fuel spilling all over him. There were no marshals present and he was lucky that two other drivers had crashed near the same spot. Finally finding his way into an ambulance, the driver got lost on the way to hospital.

If Stewart's injuries had been more severe than a broken collarbone, the results of such pathetically inadequate safety precautions could have been tragic,

Stewart in the pits at the Swedish Grand Prix, 1973

and Stewart was determined to instigate changes. His stature as an up-and-coming driver, with two Grand Prix victories under his belt, certainly helped, but he was opposed not only by the authorities, but by some drivers, who felt he was displaying a lack of courage and threatening to take the fun out of the freewheeling sport.

"It was simply ridiculous," he later recalled. "Here was a sport that had serious injury and death so closely associated with it, yet there was no infrastructure to support it, and very few safety measures to prevent it. So, I felt I had to do something."

But the criticism was virulent and personal. "It was said I removed the romance from the sport," he recalled, "that the safety measures took away the swashbuckling spectacular that had been. They said I had no guts."

It seems incredible to think a Formula 1 driver could be accused of having no guts, and equally incredible that seatbelts were not mandatory for drivers before this point. Nor were full-face visors. Stewart campaigned for proper medical teams to be present at all races and for barriers to be installed on sections of the track where cars might spin off. Formula 1 remained a deadly sport even after these fairly modest changes, but it is certain that Stewart's campaigning saved the lives of some of his fellow drivers – perhaps even some of those who had been so opposed to his crusade.

THE CHAMPIONSHIPS

Switching teams in 1968 proved a good move for Stewart. Ken Tyrrell had moved into Formula 1 and his Matra Ford was a car Stewart could compete in. He won three races to finish second, behind Hill. In 1969 he went one better, after winning five of the first six races and six over the course of the season to win his first Drivers' Championship.

As his profile increased, Stewart felt able to take stronger stands in his push for improved safety. The Belgian track at Spa-Francorchamps was particularly fearsome, as well as being the course on which Stewart had come to grief in 1966. Having walked the track in 1969, Stewart did not think it was safe enough to race on and a drivers' boycott erased it from the calendar for that year. It returned in 1970 after minor safety measures were implemented – Formula 1 was still far from safe, but was moving in the right direction.

After a disappointing 1970 season (he failed to finish eight times), he regained the world championship easily in 1971, winning six of the 11 meetings. By now Stewart was an international name, thanks in part to his rockstar looks. He was in demand from media outlets and also raced in the Can-Am (the Canadian-American Challenge Cup). It is estimated that he flew across the Atlantic 186 times in a year that finally saw his health

Stewart's rockstar looks helped establish him as the first superstar of F1

A brutal aspect of F1 in the early years, as Stewart's car approaches the burning wreckage from a major crash in Spain in 1970

crack under the pressure. A bout of mononucleosis proved he was not invincible off the track, however good he was on it.

Unfortunately, 1972 proved to be another disappointing year. Wins in the last two races could not do anything to overhaul Emerson Fittipaldi, who won comfortably. Despite poor health, Stewart had once more spread himself thin, competing in the European Touring Cars Championship as well as Formula 1.

THE FINAL YEAR

Stewart felt that his time at the top of the game was coming to an end. No doubt continuing safety concerns were a part of his decision, and the 1973 season would be his last – his career would wrap up very neatly in the United States, with his 100th Grand Prix. By then, he had won five races, taking his total to 27 and setting a new record.

His final race, however, was not to be. Stewart calculated that 57 fellow drivers had died during his career, some of them close personal friends, but none affected him more than the last, when François Cevert was killed during practice at Watkins Glen in New York.

Stewart drove another lap of the course, passed where his teammate and friend had died, and decided that was enough. He pulled out of the race and his career was over. It would take 14 years before his record for Grand Prix victories was bettered by Alain Prost.

Stewart's love for the sport was as strong as ever, however, and he worked as a commentator, a consultant and even as a team owner. Stewart Grand Prix took to the grid in 1997 and won at the infamous Nürburgring in 1999.

The sport still had a lot of love for Stewart too, even if it had taken time to forgive him for insisting on improved safety standards.

"I would have been a much more popular world champion if I had always said what people wanted to hear," he later mused. "I might have been dead, but definitely more popular."

The Nürburgring

Perhaps the most notorious of all racetracks, Stewart took immense pride in his four wins at the Nürburgring (as well as securing his only win as a team owner on its tortuous curves). But the track was also an object of dread for the Scotsman.

He remembers: "I won four times at the original Nürburgring in Germany – the most dangerous circuit in the world – and yet I was always afraid of that place. In 1968 I won there by over four minutes in thick fog and rain where you could hardly see the road. That race should never have been held, and having won it by such a big margin gave me more credibility when I demanded safety improvements."

In 1973, Stewart drove and narrated a lap at the Nürburgring with cameras in his car. The shaky footage gives an inkling of the fear the place could instil, but Stewart's words are perhaps even more chilling.

"You're going up here with so much G-forces on," he said at one point on the course, "that you can't take your foot off the throttle and get it onto the brakes."

After his lap he commented: "For a quick lap of the Nürburgring, you've probably experienced more in seven minutes and six or seven seconds than most people have experienced in all their life in the way of fear and the way of tension and the way of animosity towards machinery and to a racetrack."

Stewart flashes by in his Matra at the Nürburgring in 1969

Legendary **DRIVERS**

EMERSON FITTIPALDI

BRAZILIAN TRAILBLAZER

A mercurial driver who put South American racing on the motorsport map in the 1970s

Emerson Fittipaldi in a carefully crafted picture at the Italian Grand Prix, 1972

TOP TO BOTTOM: Fittipaldi driving for Lotus in 1971

In his McLaren suit, Fittipaldi walks in the pit lane with Niki Lauda and Clay Regazzoni of Ferrari at the 1974 Italian Grand Prix

An elegant and tactically astute driver who rose rapidly from the British Formula One and European Formula Two ranks to the F1 stage, Emerson Fittipaldi was born in 1946 into a Brazilian family seeped in motorsport. His father was a motor racing journalist, while his older brother Wilson went to compete in 38 Grands Prix, but it was Emerson who was to become the most celebrated of the sport's Fittipaldis.

Signed by Lotus for the 1970 season, he made his Championship debut at the British Grand Prix in July. He was promoted to the team's principal driver the following year in the wake of Austrian Jochen Rindt's tragic death at Parabolica in practice for the 1970 Italian GP at Monza.

By 1972 he was in his pomp, registering his maiden F1 victory at the Spanish GP in May. Subsequent wins in Belgium and Austria that year followed and by the end of the season Fittipaldi finished 16 points clear of Jackie Stewart in the final standings. He was the first Brazilian to claim the title and, at the age of 25, the youngest until Spain's Fernando Alonso broke his record in 2005.

Britain's Stewart exacted his revenge in 1973, dethroning Fittipaldi, but the South American came roaring back 12 months later. It was a dramatic campaign in 1974 that was only decided at the 15th and final race – the United States Grand Prix in New York – as Fittipaldi and Swiss 'Clay' Regazzoni arrived in America on level points. The rivals started eighth and ninth on the grid respectively but while Fittipaldi was able to battle up to fourth, Regazzoni's unresponsive tyres saw him drop back to 11th at the end of the race. The three points the Brazilian garnered, against none for his rival, saw him confirmed as a two-time world champion.

He retired in 1980 after a career spanning 149 Grands Prix but remained active in motorsport in later life, winning the iconic Indianapolis 500 in 1989 and again four years later. In 2005, at the age of 58, Fittipaldi raced at the one-off Grand Prix Masters in South Africa, finishing second behind fellow former champion Nigel Mansell.

Legendary **DRIVERS**

NIKI LAUDA

THE COMEBACK KING

Like many drivers, Niki Lauda had to buy his way into motor racing, but this three-time world champion almost paid for it with his life...

Despite having the luxury of being born into a prestigious and wealthy Austrian business dynasty (Vienna, 22 February 1949), Niki Lauda had no choice but to find his own funds to fulfil his dreams of entering the expensive world of motor racing, as his ambitions were met with unwavering disapproval from his father. After securing numerous bank loans in 1968, Lauda was able to buy his way onto the Mini team, competing in Formula Vee and Formula 3. By 1971 Lauda was eager to move on, and more importantly up, so he secured a £30,000 bank loan against his own life insurance policy in order to win a seat on Team March, racing in Formula 2, and later Formula 1.

Niki Lauda behind his Ferrari teammate Clay Regazzoni at the Italian Grand Prix, 1975

The Austrian's F1 debut came on home soil in August 1971, at the Österreichring circuit (now the Red Bull Ring), where his car failed due to handling issues on the 20th of 54 laps. Although Lauda showed great potential, it was the only chance he had to compete at the top level that season. For the 1972 season, Lauda was a fully fledged March team driver, competing in all rounds, but at the helm of a less than mediocre car he wasn't able to make the impact he had hoped.

With no qualifications to fall back on, Lauda was determined to make it work in the world of racing, so in 1973 obtained yet another loan, this time securing a seat on the BRM team. It was here his talent began to shine, gaining the attention of Enzo Ferrari, who, after a recommendation from Lauda's former teammate Clay Regazzoni, signed him in 1974.

Things turned a corner for the Austrian once behind the wheel at Ferrari, who hadn't had a Drivers' Champion in a decade. Lauda claimed his first podium on his debut race for the Italian car manufacturer – coming second in the Argentine Grand Prix, then just three races later he claimed his first F1 victory at the Spanish GP, giving Ferrari their first win in two years. He finished fourth in the championship that year, thanks to what the media summarised as a "clinical and somewhat calculating approach to driving", earning him the moniker 'The Computer'. Lauda did little to alter this somewhat cold and unsentimental persona in the minds of racing fans, and even admitted to giving away his "ugly" and "useless" trophies in exchange for a lifetime of free car

washes at his local garage. During his career Lauda was also given the nickname 'The Rat', which eventually went on to become 'Super Rat', then 'King Rat', not only due to his buck-toothed appearance, but because of his racing style, which was often described as tough, focused and tenacious.

Lauda took his first World Drivers' Championship in 1975 after some particularly gritty races, romping to victory in Monaco, Belgium, Sweden, France and the USA. After winning five races in 1976, all signs pointed to Lauda pulling in back-to-back championships, but unfortunately tragedy was waiting just around the corner.

A week before the German Grand Prix at the Nürburgring circuit, Lauda called upon his fellow competitors to boycott the race as he felt there was an overwhelming lack of safety measures in place. Most of the drivers voted against the boycott and the race went ahead. On the second lap Lauda's car, thought to have suffered rear suspension failure, veered into the track wall at full speed, where it immediately burst into flames before being struck by the oncoming car of Brett Lunger. A safety marshall rushed to the scene, along with racers Harald Ertl, Guy Edwards and Arturo Merzario, who together were able to wrestle Lauda's body, shrouded in flames, from the cockpit. Hospitalised with first to third degree burns, broken bones and lung damage due to the inhalation of toxic fumes, things looked so bleak for Lauda that a priest was called in to read him his last rites. Miraculously, however, Lauda recovered

Lauda deep in concentration at the German Grand Prix, 1975

His Ferrari engulfed in flames, Lauda is snared to his car after a terrifying crash into a barrier on the second lap of the German Grand Prix, 1976

and just five and a half weeks later, with blood seeping from bandages around his head, he finished fourth in the Italian GP. The fire from the accident led to severe facial scarring and disfigurement for Lauda. He also lost half of his ear and the hair on the right side of his head, as well as his eyebrows and eyelids. As such he began wearing his now iconic red baseball cap and, living up to his 'shrewd' media persona, secured a tide of highly lucrative sponsorship deals to adorn its front.

Although Lauda had missed two races while recovering from the accident (Austria and the Netherlands), he was still in contention for the 1976 championship, which came to a close in a showdown at the Japanese GP, where Lauda led his supposed racing rival – Great Britain's James Hunt – by just three points. Torrential rain swept in on race day and Lauda, among others, withdrew at the end of the second lap insisting it was too dangerous to continue. Later Lauda revealed the conditions were made worse by the fact his eyes hadn't fully healed from Nürburgring, as damage to his tear ducts caused his eyes to water excessively and he was still unable to blink effectively. The decision to withdraw, which saw Hunt announced as the 1976 champion, divided opinion, with some hailing Lauda as brave (Hunt included), while others criticised him for being a coward, reportedly including Enzo Ferrari, who allegedly made plans to replace him.

Using the doubt of others to spur him on, Lauda seized the 1977 championship title with two races still to go. His critics denounced his success as the result of being tactical rather than using outright pace – Lauda had finished well across the board but had only managed to secure three outright wins, in South Africa, the Netherlands and Germany, which in light of Lauda's accident was held at Hockenheimring. Nevertheless, Lauda's early championship victory saw him refuse to compete in the last two races of the season and then quit Ferrari, as friction had continued to escalate with his new teammate Carlos Reutemann, who had previously been brought in to serve as Lauda's replacement.

After Ferrari, Lauda transitioned to Bernie Ecclestone's Brabham team in 1978, where, despite having to retire the problematic car in nine out of 14 races, he was able to finish fourth at the end of the season. The following year only yielded more disappointment for Lauda, with the former champ finishing 14th, as he was only able to finish two races. After coming fourth at the Italian Grand Prix at Monza (the 13th race of 15 that season) and winning the 1979 Dino Ferrari Grand Prix, a non-championship Formula 1 race held at Imola, Lauda walked away from motor racing claiming to be "tired of driving round in circles".

Far from 'retiring', Lauda spent the following years in the aviation industry (something he would continue to be involved in for the rest of his life), running his previously founded Lauda Air, a charter airline service, where he also served as one of its pilots. Said to be in need of more funds to expand his aviation operation, Lauda returned to Formula 1 in 1982, signing with McLaren for a record-breaking (at the time) $5 million.

Although he failed to start on pole once in 1984, McLaren's faith in the former champ was rewarded when the Austrian narrowly scraped past his much younger teammate, Alain Prost, to clinch the title by just half a point. The result came down to the last race of the season, held at the updated Estoril circuit in Portugal. Championship contender Prost held strong in first place, while Nigel Mansell chased his tail in second, and current top dog Lauda moved up from 11th place on the

James Hunt and Niki Lauda share a joke in Argentina

Part of Lauda's lasting legacy was the influence and mentorship he shared with younger racing stars, including Lewis Hamilton, who he convinced to move from McLaren to Mercedes in 2012

grid to third, but that wasn't going to be enough to beat the Frenchman in the title race. Only when Mansell's brakes failed, forcing the Brit to retire, was Lauda able to move up to the second spot, clinching his third and final championship in the process.

Although Lauda retired from racing cars at the end of the 1985 season (finishing tenth), he never truly left the world of racing. He went on to work as an adviser for Ferrari (and later Daimler AG), team principal for Jaguar, a TV commentator (he was fluent in four languages), was the author of five books, and a non-executive chairman for the Mercedes F1 team. It was here that he became a mentor and close friend to Lewis Hamilton, and is credited with persuading the young superstar to move to the German constructors, where he has gone on to dominate the sport for the best part of a decade, winning six championships. Lauda, who became an International Motorsports Hall of Famer in 1993, even made a cameo in the 2013 movie Rush, which dramatised the 1976 championship battle between himself and Hunt.

Outwardly Lauda, who was married twice and had four children, seemed to be invincible, but he had to undergo two kidney transplants (1997 and 2005), as well as one for his lung in 2018. He returned to hospital in May 2019 for dialysis treatment on his kidneys, but passed away peacefully in his sleep on 20 May, aged 70. A moment of silence was held in his honour before the 2019 Monaco GP, where Lewis Hamilton and Sebastian Vettel donned special commemorative helmets. Numerous drivers, dignitaries and other celebrities attended his funeral in Vienna, paying their respects to one of the sport's greatest drivers of all time.

The 1982 Drivers' Strike

Lauda was known for his tenacity in the paddock as much as he was on the track, and one of the most instrumental things the Austrian driver did off the track during his career was to safeguard the negotiating rights of drivers. This was most notable before his first race back behind the wheel in 1982. Before the opening race of the season at Kyalami, South Africa, Lauda, along with Ferrari drivers Didier Pironi and Gilles Villeneuve, organised a so-called 'drivers' strike' after refusing to sign F1's new contract that included a clause known as the 'Super Licence', which, according to Lauda and co, made it harder for drivers to negotiate their contracts. All the drivers but one backed the strike, and refused to leave the Sunnyside Park Hotel in Johannesburg until their demands were met.

Concerned the younger drivers might be swayed overnight in their individual rooms by the F1 bosses' ultimatum of 'return now, or be banned for life', Lauda had mattresses brought into the banqueting hall, where they barricaded themselves in using a grand piano, which also served as entertainment, with drivers such as Villeneuve and Elio de Angelis tinkling the ivories to keep morale high. As there was no bathroom within the hall, the drivers were trusted to leave and return, only Teo Fabi abandoned the cause, turning tail and informing Jean-Marie Balestre and Bernie Ecclestone of the group's plans, and according to Keke Rosberg, "lost all our respect forever". The next morning the drivers' demands were met and the race went ahead with Lauda taking fourth.

Lauda in a McLaren at the 1982 British Grand Prix

Legendary **DRIVERS**

NELSON PIQUET SNR

THE FORGOTTEN CHAMPION

The Brazilian who drove under the radar to win three Drivers' Championships

Poor Nelson Piquet. His hat-trick of Drivers' Championships should see him considered a legend, but in many people's eyes he remains 'the other guy'. He'll always be the Brazilian overshadowed by the great Ayrton Senna, while British fans mostly remember him as Nigel Mansell's teammate during two tumultuous seasons with Williams. Piquet began his F1 career in 1978, driving an Ensign for a single race before switching to BS Fabrications for the next three.

His solitary finish – ninth in Italy – was enough to convince Bernie Ecclestone to give him a seat at Brabham for the final race of the season. He remained

Piquet's 1983 Drivers' Championship victory was the last time a Brabham driver claimed the title

there for the next seven years and helped steer the team from an unreliable mess in 1979 to race winners and championship contenders in 1980.

Three wins were enough to see Piquet take the Drivers' Championship in 1981 by a single point from Carlos Reutemann. After his defence ended in a disappointing 11th place in 1982, Piquet returned to the top of the table in 1983, this time two points ahead of Alain Prost.

Aware that Ecclestone wasn't paying him what he was worth, Piquet moved to Williams and reportedly trebled his salary. However, he found himself clashing with teammate Nigel Mansell. As a double world champion, Piquet thought he deserved a respect that Mansell did not show. Their infighting probably gifted the 1986 title to Prost, although Piquet made amends when he took the title in 1987 despite winning only three races to Mansell's six.

Four more seasons in F1 followed; two with Lotus and two with Benetton, where he finished an impressive third in the Drivers' Championship in 1990. In his final season, Piquet was the old hand showing the ropes to a new teammate, a rising star by the name of Michael Schumacher. Not for the first time in an illustrious career, Piquet found himself as 'the other guy'.

INSET: Piquet in his Lotus days

Piquet's championship winning Williams FW11B from 1987

Legendary DRIVERS

ALAIN PROST

LE PROFESSEUR

In an era of outstanding talents, Alain Prost managed to set himself apart

Alain Prost attracted controversy and conflict wherever he went. He was fired by two Formula 1 teams, driven out of another, and endured a toxic working relationship with Ayrton Senna. He was forced into an involuntary year-long 'sabbatical' from the sport even after winning three world championships and setting the record for Grand Prix victories.

And yet he was a thoroughly professional, calm and often affable man. If controversy kept finding him, it was because controversy came looking, not the other way around. Of course, nobody can survive in Formula 1, let alone climb to the top of the heap, without a certain amount of ruthlessness, but Prost was known for the coolness of his driving. In a sport that famously lived on the edge, and all-too frequently strayed a little too far beyond it, Prost refused to push himself to the limit. It is

'Le Professeur'. Prost lived up to his name in many a race

remarkable to consider that he might have won even more races, and even more titles, had he pushed harder. Prost, in his pragmatic way, would counter that he might not be alive today if he had embraced that style of racing.

Unlike some Formula 1 drivers, who were more or less born into a car seat, Prost was 14 before he got his first taste of competitive driving, when his father introduced him to karting during a family holiday. He was a quick learner and was a full-time racer by 1974 and a karting champion by 1975. He won championships at Formula Renault France and Formula Renault Europe before taking the French and European Formula 3 titles in 1979.

At the time, McLaren were in the doldrums after two world championships in the 1970s. Emerson Fittipaldi had won the title in 1974, with James Hunt following in 1976. With McLaren's fortunes on the ebb, Prost's victory in the 1979 Monaco F3 race earned him a test drive with the team.

It went well – although possibly a mere fable, legend has it that team principal Teddy Mayer jogged to his car to retrieve a draft contract for the Frenchman. If true, Mayer must have liked what he saw very much as he was not known for his fondness for exercise.

INTO FORMULA 1

It was an easy nickname to give a driver of slight build. Prost would become known as 'Le Professeur' later in his career, but during his first year in Formula 1, driving for a McLaren team on the verge of a radical transformation, he was 'Little Napper'. McLaren manager Tony Jardine is credited with coming up with the name, but Prost never felt quite as French as Napoleon, and would later wonder if the fact he achieved all his greatest successes with English teams was something to do with that.

Prost was an easy-going personality, which helped him ride out the ribbing from Jardine that might have rubbed another driver up the wrong way. Not only did he call Prost Little Napper, he would also shout 'get the oxygen out!' when Prost arrived in the morning, suggesting that everyone else would be fighting for air now Prost's large nose had arrived on the scene.

Although Prost would have to deal with prickly and even hostile teammates later in his career, he was fortunate in his first season. John Watson was a calm presence, much like a good-natured big brother, who did not feel threatened or jealous despite Prost's obvious talent.

Prost won his first point in his first race, finishing sixth in Argentina, and followed up with fifth place in Brazil. It was a golden era for French drivers, with four Frenchmen winning a total of five Grand Prix between them in 1980, but Prost was not among those winners. He ended the season with just five points, following two more sixth-place finishes. Encouragingly, he was just a point behind the vastly more experienced Watson.

Changes were already afoot at McLaren, with Ron Dennis and John Barnard eager to revolutionise the team. Barnard would introduce the MP4, with the first carbon-fibre composite chassis seen in the sport, but Prost would not be driving it in 1981. He was headed for Renault.

THE RENAULT YEARS

It seemed a natural fit – an up-and-coming French driver at a French team – and Prost also had a French teammate in René Arnoux, but the marriage was not a happy one. The 1981 season got off to a disastrous start, with Prost failing to finish in six of the first seven races, but his fortunes changed at his home Grand Prix. Victory at Dijon was Prost's first in Formula 1, and he followed with two more to finish the year in fifth place in the Drivers' Championship, just seven points behind champion Nelson Piquet.

Alain Prost driving for Renault in 1981

Prost had shown he belonged, but the next season would teach him valuable lessons and transform the way he drove for the rest of his career. Gilles Villeneuve and Didier Pironi became embroiled in a dispute over team orders, with Villeneuve losing his cool entirely. "He was absolutely out of control," Prost commented on the Canadian's mood at the 1982 Belgian Grand Prix.

Apparently determined to better Pironi's time in qualifying, Villeneuve suffered fatal injuries in a crash. The season also claimed the life of young Italian racer Riccardo Paletti, and Pironi was involved in a career-ending accident in heavy rain. Prost, one of the first to reach Pironi as he lay in the mangled wreckage of his car, was deeply affected.

"Everybody thinks that I don't like driving in the wet," Prost commented, "but it was almost my preference before this. I realised this day that I had to be more careful."

From that moment, Prost refused to push himself to his limit. It undoubtedly cost him time and may well have cost him wins, but it also allowed him to walk away from the sport in one piece. Prost's new philosophy on driving was in direct contrast to that of a driver like Senna, with whom the Frenchman would soon embark on a fierce and sometimes bitter rivalry. It is also fundamental to the man's 'official' nickname, Le Professeur. As commentating legend Murray Walker said: "Alain was a master tactician. He thought it all out and drove as fast as he needed to drive."

Prost himself put it a little differently, in a statement that is unusually candid for a Formula 1 driver. "I'm very realistic," he said. "I know when I'm competitive and I know when I'm not."

Of course, Prost was competitive far more often than not. In 1983, he was in control of the Drivers' Championship, winning four races and looking comfortable before his car let him down. Failure to finish in three of the last four races, coupled with a strong finish by Piquet, gave the title to the Brazilian by just two points. A turbo failure knocked Prost out of the last race, when the title was still within his grasp, and he had to settle for second place. Clearly, he was a man on the rise, but Renault needed a scapegoat for failing to win a title – and that scapegoat was Prost. He was let go from the team, but it turned out to be the best thing that could have happened.

RETURN TO MCLAREN

McLaren were entering a period of dominance. New rules for 1984 prevented refuelling during a race, and the team had an efficient Porsche engine. Coupled with Prost's considered approach to driving, it was a devastating combination that carried the Frenchman to seven Grand Prix victories.

But Prost was not alone at McLaren. He had come in as officially the number two driver to Niki Lauda and the Austrian, though not as steady as Prost, was a still formidable force. He won five races to push Prost all the way, but although the championship

Back with the McLaren team, and new teammate Lauda, 1984

was still up for grabs on the last day of the season, its outcome had actually been decided way back in the sixth race.

Heavy rain had turned the streets of Monaco into an extended swimming pool, and Prost had gestured from his cockpit that the race ought to be stopped for safety reasons. At that point he was leading but Senna, revelling in the wet, was eating up his lead at a frightening rate. The race was eventually stopped, and although Prost was awarded the win, he was only given half the usual points because the drivers had not completed at least 75 per cent of the race. Those lost four-and-a-half points would go on to prove crucial on the last weekend of the season, at Portugal.

Prost and Lauda had dominated the closing stages of the season. For the previous six races they had alternated wins – Lauda, Prost, Lauda, Prost, Lauda, Prost – but although Prost broke the cycle by claiming his seventh win of the season, Lauda finished second, just enough to snatch the title by half a point. It was the second straight season that Prost had lost the championship on the last race, and a rumour circulated that McLaren had printed posters to acclaim his first world title.

There would be no last-gasp drama in 1985. Prost cruised to his first championship, benefitting from a late-season collapse by Italian Michele Alboreto (the Ferrari driver failed to finish the last four races) to win by 20 points. As the season wound down to its rather anticlimactic conclusion, Prost took the opportunity to fly to the Vatican for a personal audience with Pope John Paul II. Although it is easy to caricature Prost as a man of science, especially in contrast to the deeply spiritual Senna, Prost was in fact a man with his own strong faith. He just did not allow it to intrude upon his racing style.

Prost had officially secured the title at Brands Hatch, in the European Grand Prix. Needing to finish at least fifth to be uncatchable, he crossed the line in fourth, although it is unclear what he thought about the wasted effort of finishing one place higher than necessary.

Prost was awarded the Légion d'honneur for becoming the first Frenchman to win the Formula 1 Drivers' Championship, but despite this, he never felt like he was a national hero. He did not court fame, and when it came calling nonetheless during his near-miss 1983 season, his response was to promptly move to Switzerland to get away from it. Even now, as a world champion, he did not feel completely accepted, saying, "Sometimes I never felt one hundred per cent French, to be honest."

Fortune appeared to be on Prost's side in 1986, although he had to cope with the tragedy of losing his brother to cancer during the season. Four racers were in contention as the season wound down, with Prost, Nigel Mansell, Piquet and Senna all in the hunt. Mansell appeared to have the championship sewn up until he suffered a blowout at nearly 200mph (322km/h) in the final race at Adelaide. That put his Williams teammate, Piquet, in position to win the championship, but Williams could not risk him also suffering a blowout and he was called in to change tyres.

Prost found himself in the lead but was worryingly low on fuel. His onboard computer said he would not make the finish line, but he defied it in order to win his second straight title, although he pulled to a halt immediately after taking the chequered flag – whether through choice or because he had run out of fuel is not known.

Prost was in dominant form in 1985, driving the McLaren MP4/2B

THE SENNA RIVALRY

In 1987, Prost was pushed down to fourth place as Williams made their move towards prominence, and McLaren were looking for a new teammate for the two-time champion going into 1988. The season did hold one highlight, as Prost won his third Grand Prix of the season at Portugal, taking his career total to 28 and setting a new record.

Prost was in favour of Senna joining McLaren for 1988, preferring an up-and-coming driver to the other hot candidate, reigning world champion Piquet. Prost got his way, but it became the embodiment of the phrase 'be careful what you wish for'. Senna immediately ruffled feathers and won the 1988 title, with Prost striking back in 1989 to secure his third championship.

Much is made of the fact that Prost was a superior politician to Senna, but it was the Frenchman who found himself manoeuvred out at McLaren. "I was driven out by Senna," Prost would later claim, "by Honda a little bit… and by Ron [Dennis]." The relationship between the two men, if anything, worsened after Prost left for Ferrari. After they collided at the first corner at the Japanese Grand Prix, knocking them both out of the race, Prost commented: "I wanted to punch him in the face, but I was so disgusted I could not do it. He revolts me."

It was a difficult time for Prost. Unhappy with the team setup at Ferrari, he fell to fifth in the Drivers' Championship in 1991 as Senna won his third and final title. Making matters worse, Prost was outspoken in his criticism of Ferrari and found himself sacked before the final race of the year. "Ferrari does not deserve to be world champion," he had said. "It is a team without directive and without strategy." Prost also fell out with the Italian media, who were highly influential, and the last straw seems to have been when he described the beloved Ferrari racing car as a "truck". To be fair, Prost was referring to the way the car handled after its shock absorbers had failed, but out of context the insult was too much for Ferrari to stand.

"Maybe the mistake I made was believing I could change the mentality, the way they work and approach problems," Prost said. Whatever the mistake had been, he was once more looking for a new team.

The rivalry between Prost and Senna certainly set pulses racing. Senna gets the best of his teammate at Imola, 1989

The battles continued for the duo, with Prost in a very competitive Williams and Senna in a less than favourable McLaren, 1993

Prost didn't have the best of times at Ferrari, seen here in 1990

THE LAST HURRAH

Prost was forced to sit out 1992, which saw the Williams-Renault team put together a season of remarkable dominance. With the team's highly advanced car taking much of the plaudits, Mansell won his first and only world title, beating teammate Riccardo Patrese into second place by a gaudy 52 points. The following season, Prost was back, behind the wheel of the all-conquering Williams car. Seven wins in the first ten races allowed him to cruise to his fourth and final championship, beating Senna by 26 points.

Knowing Senna was likely to join Williams the following season, and lacking the appetite to find yet another new team, Prost retired after his fourth title. He also felt personally hurt that so much credit for his final championship was being given to the Williams car.

Not quite finished with the sport, Prost dabbled in running his own team, Prost Grand Prix, but later admitted to getting cold feet almost straight away. Nevertheless, he pushed on long enough to rack up huge losses before deciding to bow out in 2002.

Prost had proven that a racing driver did not need to have the mindset of a First World War fighter pilot. His considered, pragmatic approach to racing, coupled with the fact that he never looked as fast as he actually was, made him less eye-catching than the barnstormers of Formula 1, but the results were unequivocal – his record of 51 Grand Prix victories would stand until 2001, when Michael Schumacher would surpass it. McLaren team coordinator Jo Ramirez perhaps summed up Prost's style best when commenting on his inspection of the two McLaren cars following the 1986 Australian Grand Prix, where Prost had won his second title: "I remember looking afterwards at the brakes on both of our cars," Ramirez said. "There was no way Keke [Rosberg] could have done another ten laps… Alain could probably have done another race… he was so gentle on the brakes, on the tyres, the gears, everything."

It was a distinctive way of driving, from a distinctive man who liked to stay within his own limits and those of his car, trusting nothing to fate. It is unsurprising, therefore, that his autobiography is titled, Maître de Mon Destin ('Master of My Own Destiny').

The early 1990s saw the continuation of arguably F1's greatest ever rivalry as old foes Ayrton Senna and Alain Prost did battle fearlessly before the final decade of the 20th century witnessed the irresistible rise of a young German driver who was to rewrite the record books

IT'S TOUGH OUT THERE 1990–99

A track favourite and feeling literally right at home, Senna in winning action at the Monaco Grand Prix, 1992

For the next two years, Senna showed what a magnificent driver he was, taking the title in 1990 and 1991. Prost, now teammate to Mansell at Ferrari, was again hot on Senna's heels in 1990, the year that Adelaide was host for the 500th Grand Prix; the race was won by Nelson Piquet. Prost and Senna became untouchable and opened up a huge lead once more. Senna was a dangerous man to have on your tail, though, as Italian Alessandro Nannini found out when he and Senna touched as the Brazilian was trying to overtake and sent the Frenchman's Benetton into the air. Senna went on unscathed to win the race. Prost's turn to be on the receiving end came in Suzuka, when Prost got in front, and Senna, desperate to overtake, sent the two of them off the track and in doing so, claimed his second title by default. We don't know what Prost thought, but it is certain that Senna's actions didn't endear him to anyone. It would not be the last time this dangerous scenario would occur in a Grand Prix.

Nonetheless, Senna was champion again the following year, again with a large number of points, 96, ahead of his new challenger, Nigel Mansell, on 72. Prost failed to win a Grand Prix for the first time since 1980. But Mansell, in a Williams by now, had given warning.

Frank Williams had only just managed to prevent the British driver from retiring, and how wonderful that he did so. Mansell gave the Brazilian a thrilling run for his money in 1991. In 1991, too, a young Michael Schumacher made such a great impression on the Benetton team that he was quickly put into one of their cars. For McLaren, it was a bittersweet triumph, because it would be another seven years before one of their cars again

Senna thankfully did most of his talking on the track, kicking off the 1990s with back-to-back titles

Mansell at the United States Grand Prix, 1991

topped the championship table; Williams was the name to watch from now on.

And it was the Williams car that finally took Nigel Mansell through to glory. And what an astonishing season 1992 was for the British driver. It could not have been better if he had written the script himself. The list is remarkable; he became unbeatable in the first five Grands Prix of the season and clocked up 108 points and twelve podiums, a new record. He eventually took nine victories having been in pole position for every race except two, was in pole position and drove the fastest lap in four races, and came second in three races, retiring from the others. He was already champion after the twelfth Grand Prix in Belgium, won, incidentally, by Michael Schumacher, who finished the season third on 53 points; a long way behind Nigel Mansell, but it was already clear that here was a driver of exceptional talent. The British Williams-Renault, McLaren-Honda and Benetton-Ford cars wiped the floor with the competition; no other car took a Grand Prix title that year and they filled the first six championship places.

Nigel Mansell and his 'Red 5' Williams FW14B were an unstoppable force in 1992

Michael Schumacher in talks with Bernie Ecclestone

Damon Hill at the British Grand Prix, 1993

Silverstone was a special race for Nigel Mansell and he ran it in fine style. Although Patrese, now Mansell's teammate at Williams, squeezed past him, the Italian sportingly waved Mansell through on the straight, and once in the lead, Mansell was not likely to give it up. Behind him, Michael Schumacher was proving that he, like Senna, would take risks to get to the finish line when he tried to force his way into a non-existent gap and collided with Stefano Modena's Jordan. Schumacher came fourth, whilst his teammate at Benetton, Martin Brundle, after a terrific start eventually came in sixth.

But Silverstone was Nigel Mansell's dream come true, a victory on home turf in his championship-winning year, which also saw him beat Jackie Stewart's record as the most successful British driver; he now had twenty-eight wins to Stewart's twenty-seven. On top of that, Mansell had led every lap from pole position and set the fastest lap before winning; it was a Grand Slam for the British driver.

It was at this point that the sport showed that ecstasy and agony are never very far away from one another in motor racing; relations between Williams and Mansell froze when Williams signed Alain Prost, and the British driver learned that Senna also wanted to race with Williams. Williams, to their eternal disgrace, offered a deal to the champion driver that he was not prepared to accept. Rightly insulted, Mansell refused and decided that for him, Grand Prix racing was a thing of the past. It was a sad end to an exceptional year and an exceptional driver.

The first of this year's youngsters to watch was Damon Hill, making his debut in the Brabham car. Hill replaced the Italian driver Giovanna Amati, the fifth and last female driver to enter Formula One. Brabham was a victim of its financial difficulties and folded after the Hungarian Grand Prix. Then there was Mika Häkkinen, who made it into the table in his second year in Formula One driving his Lotus, taking eleven points and coming in eighth. With Michael Schumacher already firmly established, the new champions were rising up through the ranks.

Alain Prost had taken a sabbatical year and was now back, driving for Williams. The rest must have done him a power of good because he now surged back to the top of the table for the fourth and last time in his illustrious career. His teammate was Great Britain's Damon Hill, and what a year he would have. A young Rubens Barrichello entered the Formula One circus for the first time and would continue to race until 2011. In 1993, his first races would be in the Jordan seat. A new team on the grid was the Swiss Mercedes-backed Sauber team. Another young driver in a Jordan seat in 1993, Edmund

"Eddie" Irvine Jr. from Northern Ireland, debuted at the Japanese Grand Prix.

The scene was set for what became the final Prost-Senna duel. And the opening race in South Africa, the last of its kind there, set the pattern. It was a dramatic race. Prost was in pole position with Senna behind him, but after a poor start, he ended up behind Senna and Hill. The still inexperienced Hill spun his car, whilst Schumacher slipped through into second position. On lap thirteen, Prost was back in second place, attempting to overtake Senna, which he managed to do on lap twenty-five. Not to be outdone, Schumacher also passed Senna. After pit stops, Senna was back in the lead, and it was when Schumacher again attempted to pass him that he touched the Brazilian and put himself into a spin that took him out of the race. Senna eventually saw Prost take his first Grand Prix of the season.

Until the Hungarian Grand Prix, the races were a tug of war between Prost and Senna; Damon Hill broke the pattern. Hill had suffered a great deal of bad luck until then, including punctures and an exploding engine, but shone as he won three races back to back. Michael Schumacher won at Estoril in Portugal. It was Alain Prost's year, however, and he drove the Williams to a cracking total of 99 points, ahead of Ayrton Senna on 73, having taken seven victories. In 199 Grand Prix, Alain Prost had won a record 51 times. With his consistency of style, he was regarded as the best all-rounder of his generation.

The sport of motor racing has seen many heroes come and go, and many of those heroes offered their lives up to the thrill of the mighty Formula One engines, those demanding and uncompromising goddesses. They may not have gone willingly, but they weighed up the very considerable risks, and they decided to take them. Yet, when the tragedies that haunt the sport are spoken of, there is one year that holds particular poignancy in the hearts of all who love Formula One.

That year was 1994.

It had all the ingredients to become a classic battle

Rubens Barrichello driving for Jordan at the British Grand Prix, 1993

Prost won the 1993 World Championship in convincing style

of wills between the upstarts Damon Hill, Mika Häkkinen and Michael Schumacher and the exotic, unpredictable, glamour boy of the sport, Ayrton Senna. It evolved to become mired in controversy and tragedy.

Senna was now at Williams, partnered with rising star Damon Hill, and another young man who rose into the top ten that year, David Coulthard.

Many changes were introduced in an attempt to curb the excessive use of technology that many thought were making drivers nothing more than puppets. In particular there was a ban on electronic 'driver aids'; active suspension, traction control, anti-lock brakes and launch control. Ironically, Ayrton Senna had commented that the season would be one with a lot of accidents because there had been no corresponding attempt to slow the speed of the cars. Refuelling was back, too, having last been used in 1983.

Michael Schumacher set down the markers from the start, winning the first two races and setting the fastest lap time on both occasions. Both Senna and Hill failed to complete the second contest.

San Marino, therefore, was an important race. It began under the most threatening of portents. Rubens Barrichello almost died in practice when he crashed at high speed. And during qualifying, the front wing came off the Simtek driven by the young Austrian Roland Ratzenberger, who was racing in his first F1 season. The car struck a wall at 195.7 mph (314.9 km/h), and Ratzenberger was dead before he reached hospital. It was Saturday 30 April 1994.

On 1 May, Senna took pole for the third time. After a shunt, the safety car came out for only the third time since its introduction in 1993, and with a rolling start, the race was under way.

Senna took the lead. After two laps, he came to the Tamburello corner at 190 mph (306 km/h) slowing to 131 mph (211 km/h).

And hit the concrete wall.

Part of the suspension struck him, and debris flew across the track. Ayrton Senna died in hospital. The

Roland Ratzenberger at a 1994 San Marino practice session with his Simtek mechanics. Little did anyone know that this would be his last Grand Prix and what lie ahead was further tragedy

Senna has inspired a generation of racing drivers

shock waves were felt far beyond the world of Formula One. The sport had lost one of the most brilliant and successful drivers it has ever known.

Heinz-Harald Frentzen was given a Formula One drive for the first time that season, in Brazil. He had impressed Frank Williams so much that he was offered the seat that Senna had left. Frentzen decided to stay where he was for the time being.

The season then fell into a pattern of Schumacher first and Hill second, but Hill eventually took six victories, so the championship would be decided in Australia. It became infamous and itself set a pattern.

Schumacher went wide at the East Terrace corner on lap 35, and brushed the wall. Hill was right behind him and able to pass, so he took the inside line into the corner. Hill drew alongside Schumacher, who suddenly turned the Benetton and aggressively struck Hill. Schumacher's Benetton became momentarily airborne and was out of the race. Hill's car, too, suffered damage and soon had to be retired. The incident looked deliberate, but it won Schumacher the race, giving aficionados a strange déjà vu sensation as it harked back to a previous year when a similar incident had given Ayrton Senna the championship victory over Alain Prost in 1990.

After the emotional roller coaster of the previous year, the 1995 season, though full of drama, fortunately produced none of the tragedies. Williams and Benetton carved up the first four places this season, and the two toughest sparring partners were again Michael Schumacher and Damon Hill. Despite Damon Hill's best efforts, however, this turned out to be Schumacher's most impressive outing to date, even though Hill won two of the first three races. Jean Alesi in a Ferrari, Johnny Herbert with Benetton, and David Coulthard also in a Williams, managed victories this season, but Michael Schumacher dominated with nine wins. Damon Hill took the chequered flag first on four occasions, but with 69

Schumacher took impressive back-to-back titles in 1994 and 1995

TOP TO BOTTOM: Taking maiden victories in 1995: Jean Alesi for Ferrari, Johnny Herbert's Benetton and David Coulthard for Williams

points at the end of the season, he was way behind Schumacher's 102.

The extent of Schumacher's dominance could be seen from his performance at Spa in Belgium, where he took the winner's podium from Hill by clawing his way back to the lead from sixteenth position. It was a masterclass in fearless, skilled driving. That rivalry between Hill and Schumacher was far from friendly; in fact, it was dangerous, as was proven at Monza when the two collided, yet again, on lap 23.

New technical regulations had been introduced this season following Senna's and Ratzenberger's fatal accidents; driver and car combined could now no longer weigh more than 1,312 lb (595 kilograms); the cars' ride height had been raised, the cockpit opening enlarged and the sides had been raised to provide better head protection for the driver; engine capacity had been reduced, fuel specifications were tested more rigorously and the size of the aerodynamic wings had also been reduced. And, inevitably, crash testing had become more stringent.

It might have seemed that the apparently aloof German driver was going to dominate the table from now on, but not so; Jacques Villeneuve, David Coulthard, Mika Häkkinen and Damon Hill had other ideas. At the end of the season, Schumacher

changed teams and went to Ferrari, which, in the short term, improved the team's prospects greatly, but diminished the driver's.

Damon Hill found himself competing that year, not so much against Michael Schumacher as against the son of another famous racing father, as he was himself. The Canadian Jacques Villeneuve was driving his debut season as Hill's teammate in the Williams, and he immediately staked out his claim to motor sport fame and glory. Fortunately, Hill was more than equal to the challenge, for he would not get a second shot at the target.

Hill set down the markers from the word go; he won the Australian Grand Prix – a milestone, as he had now equalled his father's fourteen wins – the Brazilian and the Argentinean Grands Prix back-to-back, setting a tough hill, (apologies!) for the Canadian to climb.

Villeneuve was not cowed, however, by the calibre of competition, and at the European Grand Prix, he took the lead and kept it all the way, taking the chequered flag less than one second ahead of Hill. It was nail-biting stuff. Hill had the, undoubtedly pleasurable, experience of taking on Michael Schumacher in pole position on two occasions and beating him both times. Ferrari, however, with Schumacher at the wheel, were flagging that they were back in business.

Villeneuve was proving hard to shake off, and with two races left to go, Damon Hill was only 13 points in the lead; and to make the final race even more of a death or glory show down, Villeneuve won the penultimate contest in Portugal; everything was down to the last race.

As it turned out, fate gave Hill a relatively easy ride, because Villeneuve crashed on lap 37. Damon Hill won the title and became the first son of a Formula One champion to take the trophy himself. With 97 points, followed by Villeneuve on 78 and Michael Schumacher on 59, Hill had decisively driven himself into the history books.

For 1996, sharp nosecone designs had ended their careers; blunter noses were the flavour of the season. Also, the cockpit sides had been raised again, to mid-helmet height, and there was a wraparound foam head restraint to prevent head injuries, such as those Mika Häkkinen had suffered in 1995.

Unfortunately, it transpired that the days when Damon Hill would challenge for the championship were over after he was dismissed by Williams and his seat given to Heinz-Harald Frentzen. Hill changed to the Arrows team for 1997 and then to the Jordan team the year after.

Frustrations for Hill in 1994 and 1995, paved the way for a much deserved World Championship in 1996

Jacques Villeneuve steers his Williams ahead of Ferrari new boy Michael Schumacher, 1996

Meanwhile, a famous brother had taken over the lead seat at Jordan; Ralf Schumacher.

It was left to Jacques Villeneuve to fight off the challenge of Schumacher and the born-again Ferrari 310B. Villeneuve drove a superb season in taking seven victories against Michael Schumacher's five.

Yet, they were pipped at the post by David Coulthard in the first outing in Australia, after Eddie Irvine had sent Villeneuve out of the race. Coulthard took his second victory that year, in Italy.

The greatest excitement (apart from Hill almost winning in Hungary and Ralf Schumacher nudging his brother out of the race in Luxembourg) came in the final race, in the European Grand Prix at Jerez. There was just one point between Villeneuve and Schumacher and Schumacher was leading on lap 48. Like Ayrton Senna before him, Schumacher was a fearless, and therefore on occasion, reckless, driver. On lap 48 Villeneuve spotted a gap and dived inside of Schumacher. Now slightly behind Villeneuve, Schumacher tried to stop him from overtaking and struck the Williams. Fortunately, Schumacher only succeeding in ending the race for his Ferrari, whereas Villeneuve managed to stay on the track and come home in third place. That was all he needed; he had become the world champion.

That almost repetition of the scenario played out between Schumacher and Damon Hill, led to Schumacher being stripped of all his championship points. It meant that Heinz-Harald Frentzen moved into second place and the Williams team were now first and second, with David Coulthard and Jean Alesi in joint third place. Mika Häkkinen was joint fifth with Gerhard Berger in the table at the end of the season.

Down but not out, Damon had a seat with Arrows for 1997

Victory for Villeneuve in Perez, Portugal 1997

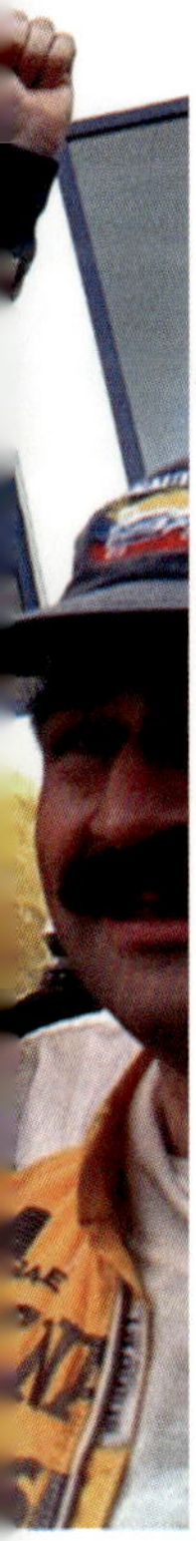

After that clash between Schumacher and Villeneuve during the last race of the season, Häkkinen took the chequered flag first; with hindsight, it was the Finn throwing down the gauntlet, and those who picked it up in 1998 had a hard time sustaining the challenge.

Villeneuve's Williams faded that year, the year that Ralf Schumacher squeezed into the number ten spot and Damon Hill got a rare look in driving his Jordan-Mugen-Honda, finishing on the number six spot. His Jordan was simply outclassed though he claimed victory in Belgium. The fight now was between Michael Schumacher, and Mika Häkkinen in the McLaren-Mercedes, with David Coulthard and Eddie Irvine battling it out for third and fourth places. Coulthard undertook a supporting role for his teammate, allowing Häkkinen to take victory at Melbourne, for example.

Changes to the rules meant that the cars were now narrower, thus reducing their downforce, and hence the speed as well.

Häkkinen took four of the first six races, winning an impressive eight in total (he didn't start at Imola and suffered a grid failure at Montréal) in comparison to Schumacher's five. The final race of the season at Suzuka had the unusual spectacle of Schumacher stalling on the grid and starting out last. In an extraordinary drive, he took himself to third place only to be defeated when debris on the track blew out his tire. Nonetheless, Häkkinen's championship was well earned with eleven podium finishes, six fastest laps and nine pole positions in thirteen completed races.

Ferrari must have harboured great hopes, however, for the following year. They were disappointed once more, because Mika Häkkinen completed a dramatic year at the front once more, after scrapping with Irvine, Coulthard and Heinz-Harald Frentzen, who suffered a fractured leg in a crash at Montréal. And suddenly, Rubens Barrichello popped back up in the table for the first time since 1996. Ralf Schumacher had the unusual

Mika Häkkinen made the most of his Mercedes powered McLaren to win the 1998 title

experience of coming home in sixth position, right behind brother Michael on fifth, thanks to the fact that Schumacher senior had broken his leg in the British Grand Prix (where Häkkinen lost his entire back wheel) and only returned with a metal plate in his leg for the final two races of the season to try and assist Eddie Irvine and his Ferrari, in his teammate's fierce challenge for the title.

Irvine won his first Grand Prix victory in Australia, led the field by 8 points at one stage, and had a 4-point advantage in the final race, by which time he had won three more. But it was not to be; Häkkinen was

Häkkinen was highly competitive for Mclaren in 1999. He took pole position in 11 races, including the Monaco Grand Prix

on superb form and became the seventh man in the history of Formula One at the time to triumph on two successive occasions.

Hopes had also been high for Damon Hill this year, but success did not materialise. True, he came fifth in Britain, but he hadn't enjoyed a good season, and retired from the sport.

One cannot help but feel disappointed that his potential was left unused after his winning World Championship drive.

TOP TO BOTTOM: **Eddie Irvine proving himself a worthy Ferrari driver**

Michael Schumacher managed two wins in 1999. His season was stalled after crashing at the British Grand Prix and breaking his leg

Nigel Mansell drives his Williams FW14 at the Spanish Grand Prix, Circuit de Catalunya 1991

"la Caixa"

Michael Schumacher enjoys the champagne at the Spanish Grand Prix, 1992

Beautiful aerial view of Senna at the Monaco Grand Prix, 1993

DOCTOR
DOCTO
31604
IMOLA

Damon Hill in the pits, changing to slick tyres after a wet Brazilian Grand Prix, in his championship winning year 1996

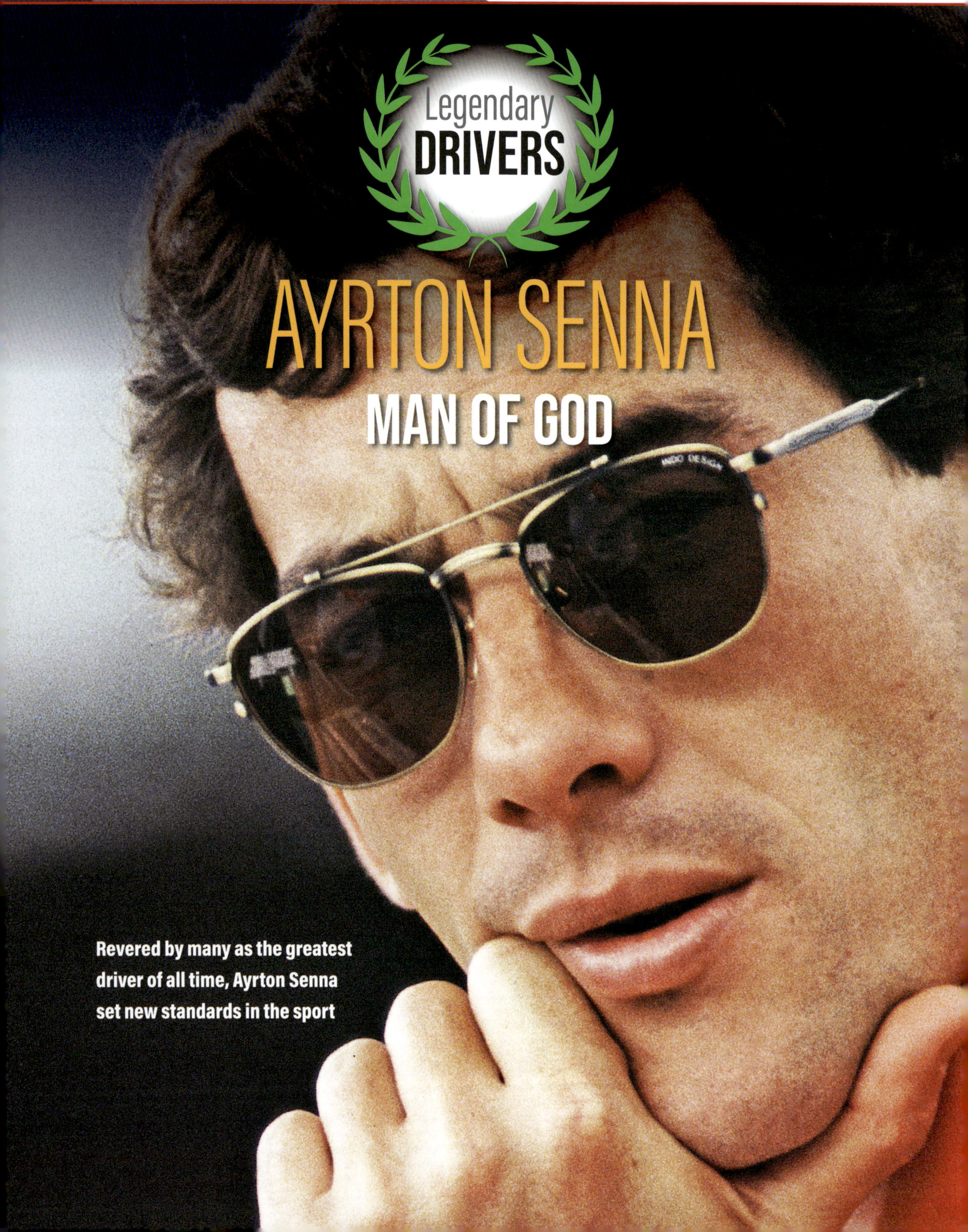

Legendary **DRIVERS**

AYRTON SENNA

MAN OF GOD

Revered by many as the greatest driver of all time, Ayrton Senna set new standards in the sport

Ayrton Senna da Silva appears to have been destined to race for a living. At the age of four he was driving karts. At nine he was behind the wheel of a Jeep. At 13, he was racing. He always knew what the primary purpose of his life was, but this did not mean he ignored all other responsibilities. He was level-headed enough to realise he needed to work hard at school so that he could devote his time to his driving when he got home.

Competing in karting, in a sport without the contaminating influences of money or politics, he enjoyed a purity of racing that he was not to find again, but his trajectory was inevitably upwards. In 1981 he won the English Formula Ford 1600 Championship and two years later the British Formula 3 title. By this time he had adopted his mother's maiden name, Senna, as da Silva was so common it did not give him the distinctiveness he desired.

Despite his parents' wishes that he join the family business, Senna was clearly headed in a different direction.

FORMULA 1

Toleman-Hart were not a glamorous name in the world of Formula 1, but with other teams not quite interested enough to offer him a seat, they would have to do. A small team with limited aspirations, they posed no threat of winning podium places or troubling the big teams of the day. Senna's debut race, fittingly enough in Brazil, lasted just eight laps, but in his second outing, in South Africa, he finished sixth to win his first Drivers' Championship point.

This first completed race was a sobering experience. Accustomed to much shorter races in Formula 3 and Formula Ford, the two hours he spent in the cockpit in the heat at Kyalami, in the Transvaal, were physically and mentally exhausting. Senna had announced himself to the F1 world, but he proved he belonged in his sixth race, in vastly different conditions.

The Monte Carlo Grand Prix saw him line up alongside such names as Alain Prost, Keke Rosberg, Niki Lauda and Nigel Mansell, all past or future world champions. Senna started in 13th place, but demonstrated what was to be one of his trademarks – mastery of wet driving conditions – as he moved up through the field. He passed Lauda to move into second place and was catching the leader, Prost, at a phenomenal rate when the race was stopped on the 31st lap, just as he was poised to take the lead. Nevertheless, a podium finish was a dramatic statement of intent.

The decision to stop the race, handing victory to Prost, was the first time the two men came into conflict in their careers. It would not be the last.

THE MOVE TO LOTUS

Toleman had given Senna his chance in F1, but it was clear he needed a bigger team. Lotus made sense

The unmistakable Ayrton Senna

TOP TO BOTTOM: Ayrton in his karting days

Senna (#1) vies for the lead against future F1 driver and TV broadcaster Martin Brundle in a Formula 3 race at Silverstone, 1983

The absurdity of the charge was made clear by Senna's team, which pointed out that exactly the same thing had happened in previous races with no sanctions being imposed.

Despite this evidence being presented, FIA president Jean-Marie Balestre stubbornly stuck to his guns, proceeding to add a $100,000 fine and a suspended six-month ban for the incident that led to the spin-off. Senna was disgusted and believed that Balestre, a Frenchman, was biased towards his countryman, Prost. He briefly contemplated retirement.

The relationship between Prost and Senna was now toxic and the two could not hope to exist in the same team for any longer. Prost left to join Ferrari, but the two exchanged bitter barbs. Senna said of Prost: "All drivers go to their limit. My limit is different from Prost's. That is the reality. And instead of trying to improve his own skills, he found it easier to attack me."

Senna in his McLaren to another race win

In turn, Prost had this to say about his mercurial rival: "Ayrton has a small problem. He thinks that he can't kill himself because he believes in God… and I think that's very dangerous for the other drivers."

In the end, Senna could not walk away from what he described as, "my aim, my target, my object, my passion, my dream, my life". He would race again the next year.

SECOND DRIVERS' CHAMPIONSHIP

The 1990 season saw Senna and Prost once more fight for the title in a championship that again came down to Japan. The two drivers had engaged in a thrilling season, each putting together devastating sequences of results to take and retake control.

Senna opened with three victories in the first five races, before Prost countered with three straight wins in Mexico, France and Great Britain. Senna responded with three wins in the next four races to build a commanding lead. As the Formula 1 circus moved to Suzuka once more, the situation was eerily similar to that of the preceding season, but this time it was Prost who had to win to keep his hopes alive.

In contrast to the drama of 1989, the 1990 Japanese Grand Prix was something of an anticlimax, but there was still no shortage of controversy. Still feeling that the authorities were against him, Senna had stormed out of a pre-race meeting when a warning against dangerous driving had been read out. Clearly, he felt the warning was aimed squarely at himself, and when alignments on the starting grid were changed, giving Prost (starting in second place) a favourable position on the racing line, Senna again complained angrily.

Sure enough, Prost took advantage of the better grip on his section of the track in order to blow past Senna at the start. In response, Senna attempted to dart through a narrow gap, the cars came together, and both men spun off. The Japanese Grand Prix was over for both of them at the first corner.

Controversy raged over the incident, but replays clearly showed that Prost had moved to his left, offering a narrow gap for Senna to attack. As Senna said succinctly afterwards, in a phrase that summed up his attitude to the sport: "If you no longer go for a gap that exists, you are no longer a racing driver."

It was a somewhat disappointing end to the season. Senna failed to finish in any of the last three races, but he was world champion for the second time.

THE WILLIAMS CHALLENGE

A new threat was emerging as the 1991 season opened. The Williams team had brought back British driver Nigel Mansell and were set to take over the world of F1, but for the time being, Senna managed to hold on to his spot. Winning the first four races from pole position suggested the season might be a stroll for the Brazilian, but as Mansell settled back into his old team, he mounted a fierce midseason charge that was in fact a warning signal for the following season. Senna held on to win comfortably, finishing 24 points ahead of Mansell to take the title, but it was to be his last world championship.

The following year, with Williams introducing waves of electronic enhancements to their cars, Senna saw his competitiveness eroded. He won pole position just once as Mansell dominated. The Brit won eight of the first ten races and Senna had no doubts why.

"When you go into this sort of electronic war," he commented, "you can find yourself completely stuck. The electronics will do the work and not the driver and I don't think that is what you want." Despite his distaste for the enhancements employed by Williams, Senna recognised them as the team to be with and attempted to switch. Williams, however, had just signed Prost, who made it clear he would not drive alongside Senna again.

The 1993 season was a replay of 1992, with Prost taking Mansell's place and winning 13 pole positions, while teammate Damon Hill won two. Senna fought heroically and won five races, but Prost could not be caught. Prost's fourth championship triggered his immediate retirement and the way was now open for Senna to join Williams.

It was always a strange pairing – Williams' team

The pressure was on. Senna knew McLaren were losing vital ground to the mighty Williams team led by Nigel Mansell

principal Frank Williams described Senna as "the best piece of equipment, in a way, you can put in the machine" – but rule changes prior to the 1994 season meant Senna never got to race in the advanced Williams car. The electronic enhancements had to be stripped out, leaving the car difficult to handle. Senna struggled with what was left, and believed that Michael Schumacher, in the Benetton, was benefitting from illegal electronic enhancements. He managed to get his car into pole position for the first three races, but Schumacher was unstoppable on the way to his first championship.

At the same time, the retirement of Prost had robbed Senna of his primary motivation. In a way, he felt lost without the diminutive Frenchman to spar against, and he even phoned his old rival to try and persuade him to come out of retirement. It was the start of an unexpected end to the men's relationship, as intense rivalry started to give way to friendship.

Where this friendship might have led can never be known, because the 1994 season would see Senna's career and life come to a shocking end at Imola, on 1 May. In retrospect, the omens were bad from the start. Rubens Barrichello was seriously injured in a crash during practice, and then Roland Ratzenberger was fatally injured during qualifying. Senna was struggling to settle in with the Williams team, and his personal life

A haunting sight. Senna leads the field at Imola in 1994, before his fatal crash

was also turbulent, as he fought to get his new girlfriend, Adriane Galisteu, accepted by his family.

On top of this, Senna had warned that it was dangerous to remove the electronic enhancements from F1 cars without curbing their speed, and his words appeared prophetic following the serious crashes that punctuated the weekend at Imola. As the race started, there was a lot on the Brazilian's mind, but he led in the early stages as he took his car into Tamburello corner. The cause of Senna's death after his car crashed at Tamburello remains uncertain, but it appears part of the car's suspension struck his helmet at just the right point to cause a fatal head injury.

Senna's body was flown back to São Paulo on 4 May for his funeral, and Prost was one of his coffin-bearers. The inscription on his grave reads: "Nada pode me separar do amor de Deus", which translates to "Nothing can separate me from the love of God."

LEGACY

Senna's rivalry with Prost not only produced fireworks on the track, but was hugely beneficial to Formula 1 off the track. The sport enjoyed a surge in popularity as the 1990s opened, fuelled in part by the compelling storylines served up by two of the greatest drivers of all time slugging it out toe-to-toe. On a smaller scale, Senna was also seen as a ray of sunshine, perhaps the only ray of sunshine, during a bleak time for Brazil. A symbol of resilience and dashing bravery, Senna gave Brazilians something to be proud of.

But of course, it is his life on the track that will be remembered most vividly. Senna was a passionate, instinctive driver. Matched against the cool calculations of Prost, he took on the qualities of a matador. Aggressive, driven and always seeking to push himself and his car to the limit, he never found the peace that he claimed to be searching for. In truth, he had probably found it earlier in life, when he raced karts in a sport devoid of politics and money. It was, in his words, "pure driving, pure racing". He never quite found that again.

Aftermath of Imola

Senna's was not the only fatality to force Formula 1 to adapt new safety protocols, but it was a seminal moment in the sport. It had been 12 years since a driver had lost his life during a race meeting, and the deaths of Senna and Roland Ratzenberger, as well as the stomach-churning crash survived by Rubens Barrichello, ushered in a new era of safety protocols. A review was initiated, and enhancements to driver safety have been ongoing ever since. It would be 20 years before another driver lost his life, when Jules Bianchi was fatally injured at Suzuka in 2014.

Improving protection and support for the head and neck were priorities after Senna's crash. This continued in 2003, with the introduction of the Head and Neck Support (HANS) device. A 'survival cell' now cocoons the driver, made of carbon fibre, which is able to resist penetration by flying debris. Wheels are tethered to stop them detaching after impact and medical teams are positioned around tracks to ensure they can reach any point within 30 seconds of an incident. Most striking of all was the introduction, in 2018, of the 'halo', which protects a driver's head from impact.

Along with improvements in track design, drivers are now able to walk away almost unscathed from crashes of greater intensity than that which claimed Senna's life.

The modern F1 car has a host of safety measures built into the car, among them the 'halo' offering proven head protection

Legendary DRIVERS

MIKA HÄKKINEN

THE FLYING FINN

A racer to rival even Schumacher, the McLaren star is a two-time world champion

Häkkinen drove for the McLaren team for an impressive eight years

The Finn officially retired from F1 in 2002. He did, however, put his driving skills to good use afterwards in rallying and in the Deutsche Tourenwagen Masters (DTM)

The greatest of the nine Finns to have graced Formula One, surpassing the achievements of fellow champions Keke Rosberg and Kimi Räikkönen, Häkkinen built his career on his fearless approach to cornering and flair for overtaking and lit up motorsport in a decade of Grand Prix action. Back-to-back Championship victories in 1998 and 1999 made him a rare breed, one of only five drivers at the time of his second triumph to have successfully defended the coveted crown.

He began his F1 adventure in 1991 with Lotus fresh from winning the British Formula Three series the previous year. His debut season was a difficult baptism of fire, but his fortunes changed when he switched to McLaren for the final three races of 1993 and promptly finished on the podium in Japan. The team made his move permanent for the following season and 'The Flying Finn' never looked back.

His maiden F1 win came at the 1997 European Grand Prix and in 1998 Häkkinen was embroiled in an epic tussle with Michael Schumacher and Ferrari for the silverware. The battle came down to the 16th and final weekend of racing in Japan, the McLaren star eventually taking the chequered flag in Suzuka, while his German rival was forced to retire, and Häkkinen was Finland's first world champion since Rosberg had opened the country's account 16 years earlier.

The 1999 season was equally titanic but this time it was the Ferrari of Eddie Irvine who was Häkkinen's principal challenger. Again it all came down to the climax over 56 laps in Suzuka and again, when it mattered most, it was the Finn who found the pace to storm from second on the grid, overhaul pole-sitter Schumacher and claim victory. At the age of 31 the Finn was a double world champion.

Denied a third successive title by Schumacher in 2000, Häkkinen bid farewell to F1 the following season. Fittingly his 165th and final appearance came at the 2001 Japanese Grand Prix, the scene of both his famous Championship coronations.

Despite the valiant efforts of Fernando Alonso and Kimi Räikkönen, who both gatecrashed the party, the first 15 years of the new millennium was an Anglo-German affair which began with Michael Schumacher's peerless five-in-a-row, followed by Sebastian Vettel's magnificent four and climaxed with Lewis Hamilton's coronation as F1's new king

FERRARI PLAYS HARD TO GET

2000-15

Michael Schumacher for Ferrari spectacularly exits Luffield corner at the 2004 British Grand Prix, Silverstone

When the cars lined up for the first race of the new millennium, the fifty-first season of FIA Formula One racing, there was great expectation in the Ferrari camp that this had to be their season. They had reason to be optimistic; the Ferrari and McLaren-Mercedes teams had dominated the championship, the previous year, excluding every other car from the winner's podium with the exception of Damon Hill and Heinz-Harald Frentzen's two wins in the Jordan-Mugen-Honda and Johnny Herbert in the Stewart-Ford. Rubens Barrichello must not have believed his good fortune when he was asked to replace Eddie Irvine in the second Ferrari seat.

Schumacher set out his stall for a haul of wins in 2000

The Williams team now joined up with BMW for their engines, whereas the BAR team had turned to Honda for their magic. The Stewart team, meanwhile, had been renamed and now started as Jaguar Racing, with Eddie Irvine as the driver. And, especially for British fans, there was a new face on the grid space and, indeed, on the table at the end of the season; it was Jenson Button, who sat behind the wheel of the Williams-BMW and made a creditable start, coming home eighth with 12 points.

From the off, Schumacher showed that he intended to take the title this season, by winning the opening three Grands Prix, and after race ten, in Austria, despite Mika Häkkinen's win, he was leading the table with 56 points to Coulthard's 50. Roles were reversed after the Hungarian, the twelfth Grand Prix, in which Häkkinen drove a magnificent race to top the table on 64 points

to Schumacher's 62. Coulthard was third with 58, but there was very little in it and all to play for. In Belgium, Schumacher forced Häkkinen onto the grass at 200 miles an hour (321 km/h); that incident could have spelt more than disaster, but the Finn recovered, drove superbly and took the race.

Italy, then, was the start of Schumacher's comeback. Frentzen caused a three-car spin with Barrichello and Jarno Trulli, and Coulthard become involved in the melée. None of the teams realised at the time that fire marshal Paolo Gislimberti had been killed when a wheel from this accident struck him on the chest. Schumacher won the restarted competition; he later broke into tears at the news, firstly that the marshal had been killed and secondly that he now had forty-one wins and had equalled Ayrton Senna's record. The final two races

Schumacher lines up on pole, ahead of David Coulthard's McLaren and Ferrari newbie Rubens Barrichello at the French Grand Prix, Magny-Cours 2000

went Schumacher's way when Häkkinen was forced to retire and then was penalised for jumping the start. Ferrari had their first championship in twenty-one years, and Schumacher was on the road to motor racing superstardom. 108 points was an impressive record.

Another piece of heart-warming news that year was that Stirling Moss, already an OBE, was awarded a knighthood.

For the next four years there was only one winning combination; Ferrari and Michael Schumacher. It was a truly remarkable success story. There were other stories, too, of course; those years contained the gradual ascent of another Finn, Kimi-Matias Räikkönen, whose fresh face appeared in 2001 in what turned out to be Häkkinen's final shot at the title. But Mika was out of luck, and perhaps it was the memory of a tepid season when he gained only 37 points that finally swayed him to jettison his helmet. Juan Pablo Montoya from Colombia made his debut this year and could be well pleased with his sixth place, and for the next few years he would prove a force to be reckoned with that others ignored at their peril. 2001 was the year that David Coulthard might have won the championship had he been driving against anyone else but Michael Schumacher in full flood. Coulthard came second, the closest he had come

Juan Pablo Montoya exits the pit lane in his Williams, 2001

MAGNETI MARELLI

or would ever come again. Ralf Schumacher finished the season fourth in his Williams-BMW and would finish the next season in the same position, which was as high as he would ever be placed on the table. It wasn't easy being the brother of a superstar, yet he did very well this season taking three victories from his brother, leaving just two apiece for Coulthard and Häkkinen.

In 2001, Schumacher lapped up another nine wins and 123 points. Yet in 2002, he even topped this by finishing either first or second in every race except in Malaysia, and even there he finished third, so that he had stood on the podium for every race that season, an astonishing achievement.

Benetton had been sold to Renault, now back in F1 racing, and Toyota had joined the fray, whereas the Prost GP team had been liquidated. It was a bad year for the Arrows team, too, as financial problems caused them to implode after the German Grand Prix. Their driver, Heinz-Harald Frentzen, had left the team shortly before, which meant frustration for him as he could no longer compete that season. But Rubens Barrichello, partnering Michael Schumacher in a Ferrari, improved on his surge upwards, begun in the previous seasons, as, indeed, did Juan Pablo Montoya in the Williams-BMW; they were rewarded with second and third placings respectively. Jenson Button got a second peek at the table in his Renault, coming seventh. Button would have to be patient and wait a few years for his turn to reach the summit.

Controversy never seemed to be far from Michael Schumacher and in Austria he was handed the victory by Barrichello, who allowed him to pass on the final lap. At the podium ceremony the crowd jeered, angered that the spirit of racing been tarnished and Schumacher's standing dropped considerably. Barrichello, Schumacher and Ferrari were slapped with a fine of one million US Dollars, but there were no rules in force as yet against such actions on the track; the fine was imposed for the failure to observe Article 170 of the Formula One Sporting Regulations regarding the podium ceremony,

when Schumacher and Barrichello had swapped trophies and Schumacher drew Barrichello onto the winner's podium. The FIA soon introduced new rules to prohibit the artificial alteration of race results.

The Ferrari-Schumacher bandwagon rolled on through into 2003, although it was a much closer-fought contest, which marked the rise of Kimi Räikkönen in a McLaren-Mercedes MP4-17 as a fierce rival for the title; just two points separated them in the season, 93 to 91, even though Räikkönen only won in Malaysia. It was the Finn's first Grand Prix victory, but it would not be the last. And there was Juan Pablo Montoya, again, tenaciously snapping at their heels. Schumacher's win this year meant that he had beaten Fangio's record, which had stood for forty-six years.

The year had its fair share of drama; monsoon conditions swept the circuit in Brazil, where Mark

Leaving the field behind, Schumacher's dominance raged on

TOP TO BOTTOM: Jenson Button in his Renault, 2002

Kimi Räikkönen in his McLaren heads Ralf Schumacher's Williams and brother Michael's Ferrari, British Grand Prix 2003

Debut winners in 2003, Fernando Alonso for Renault (top) and Giancarlo Fisichella in his Jordan

Webber's Jaguar crashed and Fernando Alonso sent tyres bouncing onto the track after he hit a barrier. Fernando Alonso was in the news again that year when he became the youngest-ever winner of a Grand Prix race, aged 22 years and 26 days, after he won the Hungarian Grand Prix, thus breaking Bruce McLaren's record. "A dream come true", as he described it.

Giancarlo Fisichella secured his first F1 win since entering Formula One in 1996, in his Jordan-Ford, one of only three career victories for the Italian. The race was abandoned with 15 laps left to go, but Fisichella was denied the joy of the podium because the prize was only awarded one week later.

On a lighter, though no less dangerous, note, the priest Cornelius "Neil" Horan ran onto the track heading towards the oncoming cars, wearing a green kilt and waving religious banners. Several cars had to swerve to avoid him and he was later jailed. Motor racing produces extremes of all kinds it seems.

Behind the scenes, the changes this year included the introduction of the HANS device. Made of carbon fibre in a U shape and sitting in the nape of the neck, it was intended to reduce head injuries, and despite complaints from many drivers, became mandatory in 2003.

The FIA also made an attempt to help the less financially secure teams by introducing one-lap qualifying as a way for smaller teams to receive more television exposure. Something even more important had changed, too. To try and prevent runaway winners taking the sting out of the competition, as Schumacher

had the year before, the points scoring system was altered so that now, the first eight finishers would be rewarded with 10, 8, 6, 5, 4, 3, 2, 1 points respectively. And Schumacher duly claimed his eighth title finishing in eighth place in Japan.

There were no such problems in 2004 for Schumacher's fifth consecutive championship, his seventh overall, when Ferrari took first and second place. Schumacher had 148 points followed by Barrichello with 140, and Jenson Button having his best year yet with 85 in the BAR-Honda finishing the season third, by which time he had ten podium finishes and one pole to his credit. The German Grand Prix might have been his had he not needed a replacement engine; that violated a new rule, and so he dropped ten places on the grid. But he still came in second, showing the BAR-Honda's exhaust to Alonso; an astonishing achievement

The Schumacher-Ferrari duo were still unstoppable, winning twelve of the first thirteen races, only Jarno Trulli at Monaco putting a stop to his run of victories after five, when Schumacher equalled Nigel Mansell's record set in 1992. That fifth win was his seventy-fifth Grand Prix victory, an impressive feat. Schumacher was denied a chance at beating the record when an incident in the tunnel at Monaco between him and Juan-Pablo Montoya ended the race for the Ferrari driver; as a collision with

Schumacher heads into the pits at the British Grand Prix in 2004, another World Championship winning year

Ralf Schumacher had done for Alonso earlier.

Brother Michael won the championship in Belgium in August, the fourteenth race of the season, by coming second to Kimi Räikkönen, after Webber had caused a pile up at the start that damaged several cars taking out four of them altogether. Apart from that sole win, you had to commiserate with poor Räikkönen; he had to endure a season that saw constant engine failures, so hopes of challenging Schumacher this year were severely dashed.

2004 was the end of the road for Jaguar Racing and Ford. Both withdrew from Formula One.

And suddenly… it was all over.

It was as though the magician had unexpectedly fallen asleep. What had happened? It was 2005. Ferrari's years-long dominance was a nightmare relegated to the past. A new era had dawned without anyone realising it. The dam had been breached and the water came flooding in.

Nineteen races were waiting.

There was a new bull in the pit; literally. Jaguar had been bought by Red Bull and became Red Bull Racing. Red Bull even acquired its own circuit in 2011 in Austria, The Red Bull Ring, which had once been the Österreichring.

Some rules changed; a restart would now take place behind the safety car instead of from a standing start, after a race had been red-flagged. Neither would the timekeeping system stop; engines were required to endure two Grands Prix without being changed.

There was another rule change that seemed to prove fatal to Ferrari, instrumental, perhaps, in their astonishing collapse. Tyre changes were prohibited during the course of a race. Ferrari used Bridgestone tyres, and their performance/reliability equation was knocked off kilter for the season. Badly. Those cars driving on Michelin tyres went on to glory.

So who were they?

Fernando Alonso in his Renault stormed the 2005 season

Spain's pride and joy, Fernando Alonso and Renault were the season's new dream team. Alonso had been in F1 since 2001. Then there was Kimi Räikkönen and his McLaren-Mercedes and then... well, way back in the distance you might have seen a Ferrari somewhere with a disgruntled Michael Schumacher at the wheel, who came forward for one victory in the US.

But the season belonged to the persistent Alonso.

The Renault was in blistering form this year and Alonso took seven victories hauling in the title with a second place in Brazil and two Grands Prix still to go. It was a momentous occasion for the Spaniard for another reason; he had won the title as the youngest-ever champion, trumping Emerson Fittipaldi; he was 24 years and 59 days old at the time. Alonso remains the only Spanish driver to have won a Formula One Grand Prix.

Kimi Räikkönen was a fierce and dangerous challenger but was dogged by engine problems yet again; three failures practically ruined his chances.

And Jenson Button had even worse luck. He was in dispute over his contract with Williams, by opting to remain with BAR-Honda, suffered a crash, had a third place written off because of a technical infringement, and had a two-race ban imposed on his BAR-Honda team when San Marino inspectors discovered a hidden fuel compartment enabling the cars to run below weight. The temptation to cheat for the glory of the podium had often proved irresistible, even if immoral. Button soldiered on for ninth place.

Alonso had no intention of yielding to Schumacher again, and as it turned out, he didn't. After a bad year in 2005, third after Räikkönen and far behind Alonso, everyone waited with bated breath for Schumacher to come steamrolling back in 2006, and it wasn't for lack of trying that the championship eluded him. Alonso and he fought like tigers all the way, providing an enthralling battle for supremacy. The tug of war moved in Alonso's favour in the early races, swinging over to Schumacher

Closely followed by Michael Schumacher, Kimi Räikkönen's McLaren fights for fifth place at the Canadian Grand Prix in 2005. Jarno Trulli for Toyota and BAR's Takuma Sato have their own battle behind

before returning to Alonso for a string of four back-to-back victories that gave him six wins and three second places from the first nine races. The tussle intensified as Schumacher went all out, and Alonso didn't win again until the penultimate race in Japan, whilst the German driver won five. Both had suffered engine trouble that had put them out of races, Schumacher's woes coming at the penultimate and crucial Japanese Grand Prix. It was divine justice by the gods of the circuit, however.

Aficionados delight in the final race being a championship decider, and this year gave them one, although neither of the main contenders won at Brazil. Felipe Massa did, the first Brazilian since Ayrton Senna to do so, and secured his second 2006 Grand Prix of eleven career victories.

Schumacher fought through from tenth to fourth at Brazil but it was not enough. Alonso took second place. At the British Grand Prix Alonso had become the youngest-ever driver to achieve a triple, pole, fastest lap and race, and now he had become the youngest driver to take a double championship, winning this year with 134 points to Schumacher's 121. Alonso had been resoundingly triumphant for two seasons, a heady achievement for the Spaniard.

By this time, everyone sensed that an era of extraordinary triumphs had ended for one driver. Perhaps he, too, had realised that his moment had passed; a driver's shelf life is inevitably limited and this driver was now 37 years old. But he had determinedly and magnificently taken his chances with both hands firmly on the wheel. The thunderclap announcement had come in Italy. Michael Schumacher, the most successful driver in the history of the Grand Prix, had called it a day.

On a lesser note, for the first time since 1956, there had been not one British constructor represented on the winner's podiums, though there was British pride when David Coulthard reached his 200th Grand Prix in Barcelona and so became a member of the prestigious '200 Club'. And Nick Heidfeld, driving for Sauber-BMW, squeezed his nose into the top ten for only the second time, the first time was 2002, coming in ninth place with 23 points, ahead of Ralf Schumacher on 20. Heidfeld's debut Grand Prix had been in the year 2000 and his third top-ten placing would come in the 2007 season when he would finish fifth.

Schumacher's sparring with Alonso extended to the pit lane at the United States Grand Prix, 2006

But if 2006 had seen the farewell of one champion, 2007 saw the birth of another. There was a 'new kid on the grid', and a kid with the attitude that Schumacher would have approved of. His name was Lewis Hamilton and he debuted that year in the McLaren-Mercedes teaming up with Fernando Alonso.

And it was quite an extraordinary and exciting first season for the young British driver not to mention British fans. Hamilton was up front from the word go, battling for the honours as part of a trio of front runners with Fernando Alonso and Kimi Räikkönen, in one of the most closely contested fights for the title that Formula One had ever seen. Hamilton's debut was even more impressive than Michael Schumacher's had been, and he came third in the season's first outing. His first winner's podium was not long in coming, and it arrived at the sixth race, in Canada, which he followed up immediately with another win in the United States, one of four that season, as the Ferraris and McLarens thrashed out the placings between them.

Another Finnish driver was making a good F1 debut that season; Heikki Kovalainen, who eventually finished seventh in his Renault.

It was a season of drama; Hamilton suffered an almighty crash during qualifying in Germany and started tenth on the grid. During a torrential downpour, the car aquaplaned and skidded off the track on lap 4; Hungary produced a 'controversial incident' between the two McLaren drivers, which resulted in Alonso being demoted to sixth on the grid. In Canada, there were four safety car starts, and during treacherous weather in Japan, Hamilton spun off the track again. It was to be another of those final race deciders, this time in Brazil, and Hamilton was leading the pack with 107 points.

The championship, then, was Hamilton's for the taking, but cruel fate determined that he would be defeated by a gearbox problem, which set him back from second to seventh place when crossing the line;

Tension in Brazil at the start of the Grand Prix, 2007. The Ferrari's of Felipe Massa (#5) and Kimi Räikkönen (#6) are ahead of Lewis Hamilton's McLaren (#2) and Fernando Alonso (#1)

David Coulthard driving for Red Bull in 2006

Hamilton leads the pack in Montreal at the start of Canadian Grand Prix in 2008

Lewis Hamilton (left) celebrates with Heikki Kovalainen after dramatically clinching the title at the Brazilian Grand Prix in 2008

that put him joint second with Alonso on 109 points, just one point behind Räikkönen. Räikkönen had taken his first title, the third of his countrymen to drive to glory. It was a bittersweet ending to an incredible season for the young British driver, who had landed nine consecutive podium finishes and set up a record for a F1 newcomer.

For 2007, it was compulsory for both compounds of tyre to be used at least once during the race. The softs were painted with a white stripe, and all cars were fitted with red, blue and yellow LED cockpit lights so that drivers would know about track signals or conditions on the circuit.

Hamilton brought more drama with him into the 2008 season, although this time, his new rival was Felipe Massa in the Ferrari, and again, it was a mighty wrestling match that would be decided by one point in the last race. A double-edged sword for British fans' nerves.

Standardised engine control units (ECUs) were compulsory in 2008, so no more traction control, and gearboxes had to last for four races.

Hamilton set down the markers in the very first race in Australia, but the next four victories see-sawed between Massa and Räikkönen. Throughout the season, mercifully devoid of too many dangerous incidents, Hamilton and Massa drew ahead until there was just the final race to filter out the winner.

Needing only fifth place to win, Hamilton kept his team and country on tenterhooks until the final bend of the final lap when he overtook Timo Glock of Toyota and claimed his reward; the World Championship. He was the youngest ever champion and the ninth British holder of the coveted prize. Truly an astonishing year for him.

Hamilton was just starting out, but another British driver, the Scot David Coulthard, decided that his time behind the wheel was now over and it was time to move on to other things. On 25 November 2008, he took over a

chair at the BBC to become a commentator for Formula One races on TV.

Although Hamilton was out of luck in 2009, British fans weren't, because this was the year when Jenson Button would shine in his Brawn-Mercedes. His shadow was going to be the German driver Sebastian Vettel in an RBR-Renault; Vettel had started driving in F1 in 2007, winning for the first time in Italy the year after and was about to take the motor racing world by storm in a way that was reminiscent of the Michael Schumacher juggernaut.

Many changes had been introduced to try and get a more wheel-to-wheel competitive edge into the races; one of these was the reintroduction of slick tyres, to decrease driver reliance on aerodynamic downforce; wet tyres were now renamed 'intermediates'; extreme weather tyres were now just 'wet' tyres. Front wings were lower and wider, with the rear wings higher and narrower. Finally, to improve the downforce and aid overtaking, adjustable front wings were permitted.

So, armed with eight engines to last the season, the teams launched into a struggle between Button in the Brawn-Mercedes and Vettel in the Red Bull-Renault. Of the two Brits out there, it was crystal clear who was determined to grab the limelight this time. Jenson Button took the first race in Australia, and so Button and Brawn-Mercedes became the first team to start on pole and win the race on their debut since Mercedes-Benz in 1954. A double of sorts for Mercedes.

After a messy start in which Button got clean away, the British driver soon opened up a four second lead, with Vettel in pursuit and Hamilton working his way up from eighteenth position to ninth. Button took his pit stop on lap 19 and came out ahead, driving well and in no danger. It was Vettel who hit a wall and damaged his wheel towards the end, and with debris on the track, this led to only the second safety car finish in Formula One

Jenson Button in the Brawn leads Felipe Massa's Ferrari and Red Bull's Sebastian Vettel at the Spanish Grand Prix, 2009

racing. Button had secured his first spectacular win and delivered his warning. If you can't beat me, you're not in with a chance.

Vettel took up the challenge but couldn't get to the line first until the third race, after which he saw nothing but Button's tail for the next four outings. At twenty-nine years of age and a decade in major league motor racing, Button eventually finished with 95 points to Vettel's 84, and took the crown, Britain's tenth World Champion. Proof that with the right hardware, a good driver can always excel.

New kid on the grid this year was Bruno Senna, the nephew of racing legend Ayrton Senna. But history would not repeat itself in the same family as far as talent was concerned, and after the 2012 season, during which he completed the fastest lap in Belgium, Senna's F1 career was over when Williams dropped him.

2010 turned out to be a cracking year, although the two British drivers were shown the back seat by a dynamic Vettel and an Alonso resurgence. Not for want of trying did they only manage fourth and fifth places; Button hit the winner's podium twice and Hamilton three times. In fact, the top place was wrenched back and forth between drivers no less than nine times over the course of the season. Until midway through, it was uncertain whether Red Bull, Ferrari or McLaren would be ultimately victorious. Mark Webber, Vettel's partner, was having a great season in his Red Bull, too, and took four victories. Webber had been in F1 since 2002 and scored his first victory in 2009, one of eight podiums.

Resentment in a second driver often bubbles to the surface if they feel they are being given less attention, and this year, the problem surfaced between Vettel and Webber and also Alonso and Massa. As the season drew to a close and the inter-team rivalry became verbal, Red

Sebastian Vettel claimed victory at the Malaysian Grand Prix ahead of Red Bull teammate Mark Webber and Nico Rosberg's Mercedes

The comeback kid. Michael Schumacher had a new lease of F1 life with Mercedes

Bull insisted that its drivers were free of team orders and could do as they wished, whereas Alonso was favoured without a second thought by Ferrari. This benefitted the Spaniard, because with just two races left to go, he topped the table eleven points clear of Webber, with Massa having fallen a long way down. By the last race in Abu Dhabi, the title was up for grabs by three drivers; Vettel, Alonso and Webber. Hamilton would have needed divine intervention to join them.

Just for the record, it wasn't forthcoming.

Vettel had to come ahead of Alonso by sixteen points to take the title; it was a Herculean task, but when the unfortunate Spaniard got stuck in midfield, Vettel took off and was only seen by his rivals again after the flag. It had been a record season for the young German. Young he was; in fact, he had now assumed the title of the youngest World Champion, at the age of 23 years and 134 days.

Vettel had beaten his fellow German Michael Schumacher that year; Schumacher had decided that he wanted another bite at the cherry and was convinced that he could grab that eighth title. He had overestimated himself, and fourth would be his best position before he called it a day once more; the young drivers were sharper and faster, even though Schumacher was still his old ruthless self and almost shoved Barrichello into a wall.

The Vettel steamroller drove onwards for the next three years, and it seemed as though the German might emulate Schumacher, so untouchable he seemed to be. Everyone hoped that if that was to be the case then at least there would be exciting challenges to look forward to, for no one wanted a repeat of the deadly certainty of those Ferrari years. And indeed, Vettel was looking over his shoulder during those years, first at Button and then at Alonso, with Australian Mark Webber biting everyone's heels.

But Vettel continued his domination of the table with an impressive 2011 season in which he lost only two of the first eight races, conceding to Lewis Hamilton and then Jenson Button. Only Webber and Alonso were also able to take a race apiece. At Brazil, the final race of the season, Vettel broke Nigel Mansell's record by taking his fifteenth pole position, and he became the youngest driver to take a second championship; 24 years and 98 days old.

For the next two years, it was left up to Alonso to try and unseat the champion, although seven different drivers took one race each in the early part of the 2012 season. Pirelli had now taken over the tyre manufacture for F1, but the rapid degradation of their compounds on the track was causing problems.

Although Alonso eventually took three races in 2012 and Button and Hamilton took three and four apiece, four consecutive wins starting in Singapore brought Vettel back into the running, so that the last race in Brazil would be the decider. It went to Jenson Button, who was too far back in the title race, however, to make a difference at the top.

Many felt that Alonso had been the driver of the season, but he was destined to be runner up when Vettel came in sixth to claim his title for the third consecutive year and as the youngest driver to make that triple.

Pushed out of the table altogether, Michael

McLaren driver Jenson Button celebrates a win at the Hungarian Grand Prix in 2011, with Vettel second and Alonso third for Ferrari

Schumacher could now see that his moment had passed and he retired again.

Lewis Hamilton had wanted a new challenge and Mercedes welcomed him into their corner to fill the seat Schumacher had vacated.

Footnote to the season; Mexican Sergio Pérez squeezed his Sauber-Ferrari onto the table in tenth place this year. Pérez had debuted in 2011.

The Vettel steamroller thundered on throughout 2013 giving the driver his most decisive victory to date; 397 points to Alonso's 242. Vettel won the championship for the fourth consecutive season with four races still to complete, only the third driver in sixty-four years of Formula One to do so. He eventually took thirteen of the nineteen races, with nine consecutive wins to finish the season, a spread to equal Alberto Ascari's record of 1952/53. To the despair of everyone else, he seemed as unassailable in his Red Bull-Renault as Schumacher had been in his Ferrari. But the tensions between Webber and Vettel boiled over when Vettel ignored the team's instructions to Webber's detriment. Upset at what he considered to be the preferential treatment afforded to Vettel, Webber left F1 racing at the end of the season.

F1 now bid farewell to the 2.4-litre V8 engine configuration that had been used since 2006. For the new season of 2014, a 1.6-litre turbocharged V6 engine

The Sebastian Vettel Red Bull onslaught continued

Now sat behind the wheel of a Mercedes, Lewis Hamilton got to grips with his new car and teammate Nico Rosberg who was a an old sparring friend

formula would be used. It was hello to Russia for the first time in a century when the sixteenth race of the season was held at Sochi. New rules meant that engines had to last for at least 2,500 miles (4,000 km) before being changed and the minimum weight of cars was now 1,415 lbs (642 kg) to 1,523 lbs (691 kg). Scarily, there would now be double points for the final race of the season.

What would 2014 bring? Everyone knew what to expect.

What no one expected was to see Vettel humbled; and yet that was the scenario. It was one of the most extraordinary upsets in F1 history, with Vettel squeezed off the winners' podiums completely, and the man who did the squeezing was former champion Lewis Hamilton.

Both he and Vettel were forced to retire in the first race, so no one was any the wiser about what was going happen. But from Malaysia on, beginning with four consecutive wins, Hamilton stormed to a magnificent eleven victories, holding off repeated challenges by his teammate Nico Rosberg to do so. Mercedes took all except three victories, because Rosberg took five races and came second that year. 384 points saw Hamilton take his second championship with Rosberg second on 317, and way above Vettel in fifth place with 167.

There had been two, almost new kids on the grids this year; Daniel Ricciardo had climbed into Webber's old seat for Red Bull and kept the team's flag flying by driving a terrific season and finishing in third place. Finnish driver Valtteri Bottas had a great season too, coming fourth with Williams.

One accident left the 2014 F1 season with a tragedy, the first fatal accident since 1994. Frenchman Jules Bianchi lost control of his Anglo-Russian Marussia in extremely wet conditions, and he collided with a recovery vehicle, during the Japanese Grand Prix. He went into a coma from which he never recovered and died on 17 July 2015 after spending nine months in a coma

Sebastian Vettel (left) ignores team orders at the Malaysian Grand Prix in 2013, to overtake Mark Webber. The atmosphere was high post race, with Webber saying to Vettel "Multi 21, Seb. Multi 21"

Hamilton leaving McLaren was a risk that ultimately paid off after winning the 2014 World Championship in style

following the accident. It was a terrible and painful reminder of what danger the F1 driver finds himself in for the duration of every race.

So with the tables turned, in 2015 Hamilton was the boy to beat and he proved a hard nut to crack, leading the table ahead of Rosberg and Vettel, in a season that was primarily a supreme battle between these three superb drivers. Valtteri Bottas made his presence felt and Kimi Räikkönen and Felipe Massa proved that they are also first class drivers, as did the Russian Daniil Vyacheslavovich Kvyat – who first raced in Formula One in 2014 and now partnered Daniel Ricciardo. These were the drivers who eventually filled the first seven places on the table. After a great season, Kvyat was just able to hold off his teammate and finish on seventh place.

Vettel was within three points of the lead at one stage in the season, and one of the most remarkable races took place when the teams lined up in the United States on the 25th October; Hamilton was 66 points clear of Vettel on the table. The track was wet, there was a collision involving Massa and Alonso on the first lap, and only twelve cars were destined to reach the finish line. Hamilton and Ricciardo battled for the lead until

TOP TO BOTTOM: Red Bull's Daniel Ricciardo fends off Williams driver Valtteri Bottas at the Hungarian Grand Prix, 2015

Newcomer Max Verstappen in his Toro Rosso, 2015

Rosberg managed to get in front on lap 18; he was still there on lap 27. Another collision on lap 36 then took out Ricciardo and Hülkenberg. On lap 43 it was Daniil Kvyat's turn to have an accident.

All efforts by the other leading drivers were in ultimately in vain, however, after Rosberg lost the lead to Hamilton on lap 48 when his rear wheels started to spin causing him to slide off the track.

Lewis Hamilton had taken control of the racetracks for the third consecutive year and after eleven pole positions, he claimed his third World Championship by winning the USA leg of the competition with three races still to go, decisive proof that Hamilton is one of the top drivers of all time. Hamilton eventually took 381 points to Rosberg's 322 with Rosberg winning the final three races of the season.

F1 masterclass. Lewis Hamilton speeds out of a corner at the Australian Grand Prix, 2015

Take me for a ride, rain master! Michael Schumacher at the European Grand Prix, Nürburgring 2000

Fernando Alonso in his Renault holds off the challenge of Schumacher in his Ferrari at the Bahrain Grand Prix, 2006

Celebrations for Alonso after beating his rival Michael Schumacher (left) at the Bahrain Grand Prix in 2006

GIVES YOU WINGS
Red Bull

Vettel concentrates before taking his next lap in testing for Red Bull in Valencia, Spain 2009

TOP TO BOTTOM: Lewis Hamilton's McLaren pursued by Ferrari's Felipe Massa, Japan 2011

Vettel bows to his Red Bull after clinching the Indian race in 2013

Ferrari pit stop for Fernando Alonso, Italy 2012

TOP TO BOTTOM: Max Verstappen attends a seat fitting in free practice for Toro Rosso, Japan 2014

Lewis Hamilton celebrates with the Mercedes team, USA 2015

Legendary
DRIVERS

MICHAEL SCHUMACHER

THE RED BARON

Ruthless, dedicated, determined - Michael Schumacher was all of these, which is perhaps why he is one of the best drivers ever in Formula 1

Is Michael Schumacher the GOAT (Greatest Of All Time)? Lots of people certainly claim he is, and those who do argue that the sheer weight of his achievements overwhelms any thoughts that possibly Ayrton Senna or Alain Prost were more artistic, or that Juan Manuel Fangio was the best, albeit in an entirely different era. But if statistics are the only measure, then Lewis Hamilton has equalled or broken most of Schumacher's records.

Hamilton now has the same number of world titles and has more race wins, more podium finishes and more points (even when adjusted to the current era). So where does that leave Schumacher in the all-time rankings? Still pretty close to the top, although the GOAT title is always going to be a subjective one. It's not just because of his seven world championships – won for two different teams – but his five-in-a-row for Ferrari is still a record that even Hamilton is unlikely to beat. For a period, Schumacher was nigh-on unbeatable when it really mattered.

It all began in the same manner in which many drivers take their first steps – karting. For Schumacher, though, it was often a case of make do and mend; he never had the money to afford the best karting equipment so he had to buy and borrow what he could. Although his father, Rolf, ran the kart track where the family lived, he was a bricklayer by trade and money was never plentiful. He claims he never had any long term plan about progressing through the various forms of racing, or that he ever really thought about Formula 1. He just went karting because he enjoyed it, and found he was good enough at it that people were prepared to pay him to do it. In fact, so much did Schumacher enjoy karts, that even as F1 world champion he would sometimes spend time in the off-season racing them, or testing the tyres on them, for free. Part of it is that Schumacher is obsessive over details, whatever vehicle he happens to be in. Reams have been written about the German ace's involvement in the smallest details, such as how, when at Benetton, he had a speedometer in his car so he could check for himself which was the quickest racing line to take. And once he got to Formula 1 he loved all the driver aids, such as traction control, and would spend many hours tinkering and fine-tuning until he was satisfied that he had maximised their advantages.

Schumacher took winning in his stride

Michael Schumacher racing karts in Kerpen, Germany, 1994

Ross Brawn once indicated that Schumacher was so good he could manoeuvre round any problem. "We actually learnt more from [the likes of] Eddie Irvine or Rubens Barrichello," he said. "With them, we could always tell if there was a problem by looking at lap times." Schumacher, on the other hand, would be fast and consistent even when there was an issue – he would just work out ways around it.

A RACING LIFE

But first, let's backtrack a little. Schumacher won the German kart title before he even held an official karting licence (too young to apply for a German licence, he got one in Luxembourg instead). By 1987, he was the European kart champion as well, and the following year, he made his first debut in single-seat car racing by participating in the German Formula Ford series.

In 1989, Schumacher signed with Willi Weber's WTS Formula Three team and competed in the German Formula Three series. Thus began a lifelong association with Weber, who owned a management company and became Schumacher's manager. Schumacher won the Formula Three title in 1990 and the same year he joined the Mercedes junior racing programme in the World Sportscar Championship. This was an unusual step, recommended by Weber, who thought that long-distance races in powerful cars would benefit Schumacher's career. He only ever competed in one Formula 3000 race, considered the more obvious route to F1 for aspiring drivers. That was in the Japanese Formula 3000 Championship in 1991; he finished second. He also drove in Le Mans that year as it was part of the World Sportscar Championship, finishing fifth with teammates Karl Wendlinger and Fritz Kreutzpointner.

Schumacher's F1 debut came about in the strangest of ways, at the 1991 Belgian Grand Prix. Jordan driver Bertrand Gachot was convicted of actual bodily harm following an altercation with a taxi driver who he sprayed with CS gas. Although Gachot's initial 18-month sentence was later reduced to two months, it left team boss Eddie Jordan searching for a replacement driver at short notice. Schumacher got the nod, and immediately impressed. It is occasionally forgotten that his race actually only lasted until the second corner, when mechanical failure in the Jordan ended it. However, it was in qualifying that Schumacher caught the eye. He qualified in seventh, which was a season's best for a Jordan and higher than the experienced Andrea de Cesaris managed.

Jordan saw Schumacher was a star in the making, and tried to sign him. Unfortunately for the maverick Irishman he was far from the only team boss to realise that, and the flamboyant Flavio Briatore snatched him away for Benetton at the 11th hour.

F1 STARDOM

Schumacher's move into Formula 1 was complete at the start of the 1992 season, but for the next two years it was Williams who dominated, not Benetton. Not only did they have a supremely fast car powered by excellent Renault engines, they also had one fully equipped with semi-automatic gearboxes and active suspension. It wasn't until 1993 that Benetton introduced their own

Schumacher at the wheel of a Benetton, British Grand Prix, 1993

active suspension and traction control, the last of the major teams to do so. In 1994, it looked like Benetton had cracked it, with Schumacher winning six of the first seven races (and finishing second in the other). But then disaster struck. Benetton were investigated for breaking the governing body's new rules on electronic aids. They were eventually exonerated, but only on the technical grounds that there was no evidence that the form of launch control software found, which was illegal, had actually been employed.

Next, came the first signs of Schumacher's desire to win at all costs. First he was disqualified from the British Grand Prix for ignoring a black flag, and banned for two races. Then, on his return, he was disqualified from the Belgian Grand Prix, after winning it, for illegal wear on the skidblock. (The skidblock is a 10mm thick wooden plank which prevents the cars from running low enough to contact the track surface; this skid block is measured before and after a race and if it's found to be less than 9mm thick after the race, the car is disqualified.)

Schumacher missed the next two races, in Italy and Portugal, which enabled Damon Hill to close the gap at the top of the standings to just a single point going into the final race in Australia.

Schumacher was always in front of Hill in Adelaide, but the Briton kept sufficiently close to maintain the pressure and on lap 36, the German ran too wide on a left-hand corner and hit the wall. His race was over, Hill would be the champion. Except as Hill came round the same bend a couple of seconds later, Schumacher hit him and Hill's Williams was also too badly damaged to continue. Was it deliberate? It's impossible to say for certain, however many times one watches the replay. Hill was certainly magnanimous in defeat, saying he needed to get two points to become world champion, and didn't. End of story. Others were less sanguine, with British fans and the British media opining that it was a

Michael Schumacher in 1994 Benetton action

calculated move. Hill was hugely popular in the UK, and this incident might have been coloured by the general perceptions of the two men.

It was a different story in 1995. Schumacher was in control more or less throughout the year, winning his second world title and also helping Benetton to the Constructors' Championship for the first time. It was clear Benetton couldn't hold onto their prize asset; Schumacher looked around and, in typically clinical fashion, decided that Ferrari offered him the best opportunity.

THE FERRARI YEARS

A year after he had signed for Ferrari, Schumacher managed to lure Ross Brawn and Rory Byrne into following him, reuniting the 'dream team' from Benetton. Jean Todt had been team boss since July 1993, and together these four men set about making Ferrari great again. Todt's genius lay in uniting a previously fractured team, though the car itself remained stubbornly uncompetitive for Schumacher's first couple of seasons.

Schumacher was fast, undoubtedly, but the Ferrari was not yet reliable enough over the course of a long season. Schumacher won races and in 1999 he helped Ferrari to their first Constructors' Championship since 1983, but a broken leg suffered at the high-speed Stowe Corner at Silverstone ruled him out for three months and cost him a realistic shot at the Drivers' crown.

It wasn't until 2000 that the entire package came together and swept Schumacher to his third title, and his first with Ferrari. Four more were to follow over successive seasons, with Ferrari also taking the Constructors' title on each occasion. Schumacher said later that the 2000 title was the one that mattered: "[It] is the one that means the most to me. Everything that came after was a bonus." Schumacher could never exactly be described as carefree, but certainly it appeared that a weight had been lifted. The next three seasons saw Ferrari in charge, and Schumacher recorded 39 of his 91 Grand Prix victories over the

It took the dream team of Jean Todt (right), Ross Brawn (left) and Schumacher a few years to work out Ferrari's problems – and solve them in spectacular fashion

Ferrari crushed all the opposition in 2004

Schumacher at the Canadian Grand Prix, 2005

period from 2001 to 2004. But it was the 2004 season when we witnessed driver and car in perfect harmony. Schumacher won 12 of the first 13 races in the championship that year, missing out only in Monaco where he clashed with Juan Pablo Montoya. He added another triumph in Japan, meaning he had won 13 out of 18 races; since teammate Rubens Barrichello won in Italy and China. There were only three races in the entire season that were not won by a Ferrari. This is an almost unbelievable level of consistency, particularly for a car that only a few years earlier was the epitome of unreliability.

RETURNING TO THE MOTHERLAND

Intriguingly, there was a time when Schumacher thought his Ferrari years were only one part of his career. As a former Mercedes junior, and a German to boot, the lure of the marque was significant and a serious approach was made in 1998. But ultimately, Schumacher and Todt made a good team – they were similarly work-obsessed and had the same views on how an F1 team functioned. On the other hand, Ron Dennis at Mercedes had a slightly different style, about which Schumacher said: "There might have been a way to work with Mercedes, but not with Ron Dennis. Our points of view on how a team works were just too different." It was not until Schumacher came out of his first retirement (which lasted four seasons) that he eventually made the journey back to Mercedes.

By then it was a new team, with Ross Brawn as team principal. Many felt Schumacher might be past it, though Damon Hill warned, "you should never write Schumacher off." As it turns out, he was not able to add to his tally of race victories in his three seasons with Mercedes; the car was not comparable with the Red Bull that dominated the Constructors' Championship in those years. It was frustrating for such a born winner as Schumacher to be held back by inadequate cars, and by the end of the 2012 season he retired for good. Hamilton replaced him, going on to equal or break many of Schumacher's records over the next seven years, in the Mercedes.

Mercedes tempted Michael back into F1, with mixed results

THE SCHUMACHER STYLE

There are so many examples of Schumacher's phenomenal skill that it's impossible to pick them all out. His 1995 victory at Spa when he started in 16th. His first win for Ferrari in 1996, when he mastered the pouring rain and showed for the first time what a threat he was going to be in bad weather conditions. The 1998 Hungarian Grand Prix where he made up 25 seconds in 19 laps to take victory. The Malaysian Grand Prix in 2001, which he won despite a catastrophic 72-second pit stop. And then there were the duels with other fine drivers: Damon Hill, Gilles Villeneuve, Mika Häkkinen, Fernando Alonso – all of them world championship-winning drivers themselves.

How much did these victories owe to Schumacher's single-mindedness? The psychology of Michael Schumacher is an interesting study. As has been mentioned, he liked to be closely involved with all aspects of preparing and testing a car, and he often talked about being one part of a highly skilled team that was chasing the same dream. His perfectionist tendencies were all too clear, and he has spoken of how he approached every corner with the intention of taking it on as fast as was humanly possible. Rival drivers have pointed to his ability to compartmentalise and focus utterly on the task at hand.

Hill, who competed against Schumacher more than most, once said that Schumacher seemed able to shut off his emotional side while in a car and bend it to his iron will. "If sport is to have any worth, then there are certain human values which have to be observed. It is only then that a victory or a championship can be rated as a great achievement," said Hill. "I think that idea baffles Michael."

Take a look at Schumacher as he strides towards his car on race day, locked and loaded. Totally focused. Taking a car to its limit is just what he does, it comes so naturally to him that – like a lot of world-class sportspeople – he can't actually put it into words. He can't explain what he is feeling, because he isn't actually feeling anything except a oneness with the car. Schumacher himself has offered the opinion that what he could promise was "consistency. Lap times weren't good one day then bad the next. I believe the information I provide needs to be clear and rational, not clouded with emotion."

A LASTING IMPACT

Looking back at Schumacher's career, it's interesting to examine what impact he had on Formula 1. His legacy to Ferrari is that he made them great again. It is as simple as that. For the world's greatest car marque, and the most successful F1 team of all-time, it was vital that they got back to winning ways after a painful period in the wilderness.

On a more personal level, Schumacher undoubtedly sparked German interest in F1. Previously something of a niche sport in his home country, it became hugely popular and even though he moved his family to Switzerland to avoid the punitive tax regime in Germany, Schumacher always enjoyed the support of his fellow Germans. When he retired for the first time, in 2006, three of the top ten drivers in that year's standings were German. Sebastian Vettel, himself a four-time world champion, has said that Schumacher was a key inspiration for his own F1 career.

The tragic skiing accident that almost killed Schumacher in 2013 is not a conclusion befitting one of the greatest of sportspeople. Fans of F1, of motorsport and indeed sport of any kind will know that this colossus of racing deserves so much more than that.

Schumacher could lend his style to most modes of transport

The son also rises

The awful fate that befell Michael Schumacher on 29 December 2013 in Méribel in the French Alps has had a profound effect on the sporting world. In more recent years we have seen fatal accidents in F1 all but eliminated, so it seems deeply ironic that one of the greatest of all time suffered his worst injury away from the track. His son Mick, 14 at the time, was with his father that day and was already a racing driver. Keen not to be seen to be cashing in on the family name, or the privileges it might bestow, Mick Schumacher began his career using his mother Corinna's maiden name of Betsch. Like his father, he had started in karts before moving successfully through Formula 4, Formula 3 (winning the European title in 2018) and Formula 2, which he won in 2020.

Mick made his Formula 1 debut for Haas in the first race of the 2021 season, the Bahrain Grand Prix, and continued with the team through 2022. Haas was, sadly, not competitive but he managed to secure 12 points from 43 races, with his best result a sixth-place finish at the 2022 Austrian Grand Prix. In 2023, Mick signed for Mercedes as reserve driver. Perhaps more significantly, he also served as reserve driver for Ferrari from 2019 to 2022 – expect to see him driving for the Prancing Horse his father did so much to revitalise before too many seasons are out. It would be a very welcome codicil to the Schumacher story.

TOP TO BOTTOM: Mick has shown great promise, but has so far not quite lived up to his fathers glittering career

Driving for the Haas team in 2022

Legendary
DRIVERS

FERNANDO ALONSO

F1'S KING OF CONTROVERSY

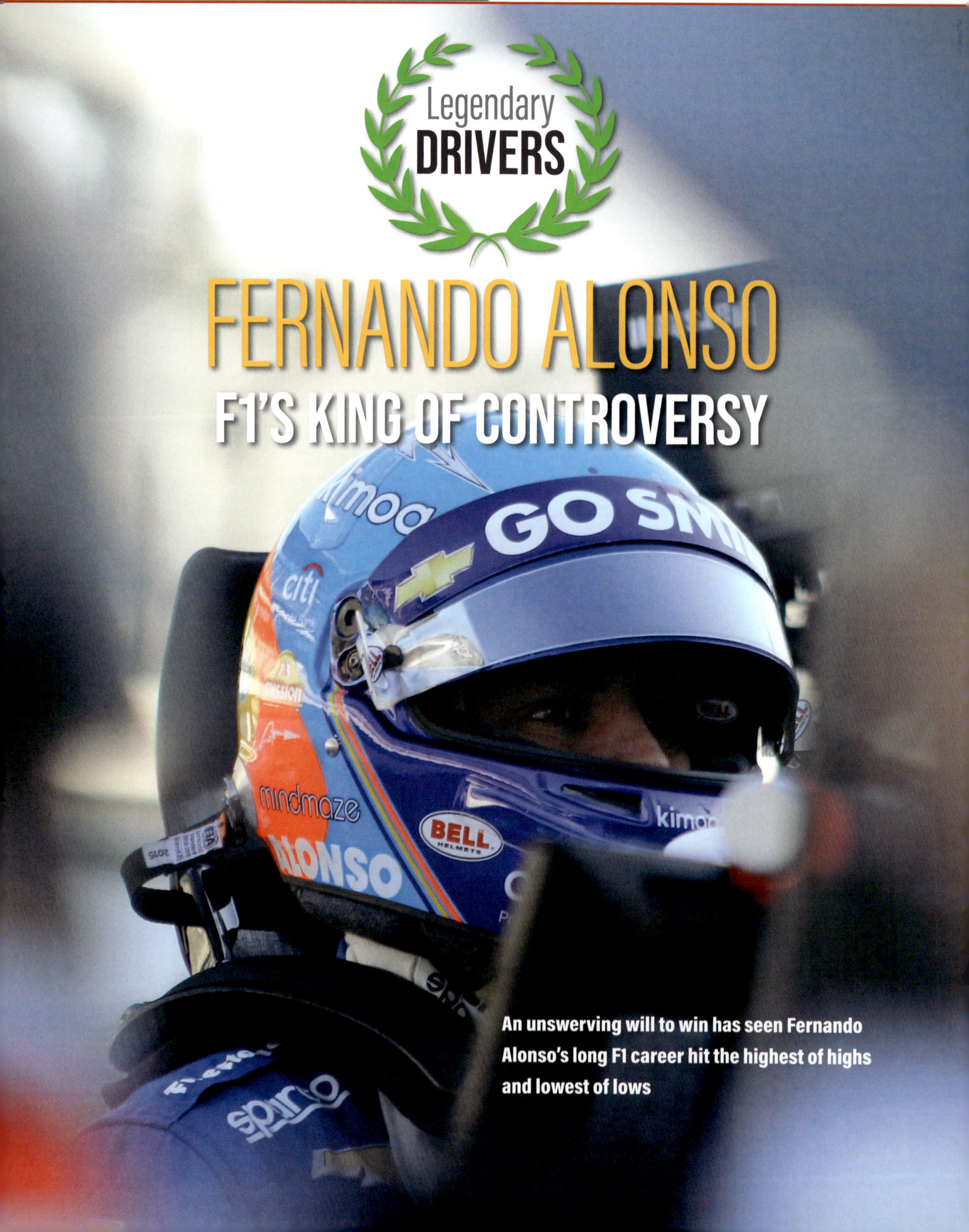

An unswerving will to win has seen Fernando Alonso's long F1 career hit the highest of highs and lowest of lows

You don't win two F1 world titles without talent, and Fernando Alonso certainly has that in abundance. But there are so many more subtle – and not so subtle – nuances that take him to another level. Aggressive, uncompromising, a fighter and having a laser-like focus on winning are reasons enough for his success. But he also brings consistency, intelligence, adaptability and, some might say, petulance, to his driving game.

However, the true measure of this exceptional man comes from his F1 peers, who simply describe him as the closest they have seen to the complete racing driver.

Born on 29 July 1981, in Oviedo, northern Spain, his father was a keen amateur kart racer who shared his passion with his children. It wasn't long before three-year-old Alonso was jumping into a hand-built F1 lookalike pedal cart. The seeds had been sown and shortly after his seventh birthday, he entered his first proper kart race and won. He continued to rise through the karting ranks and by the time he reached his mid-teens he had a karting world championship under his belt. He knew he was good and wanted more.

In 1999, aged just 18, he got his first go in a Formula 1 car at a test session at the Circuito de Jerez, part of a deal for winning a Spanish-based single-seater championship. After this, he knew exactly where he wanted to be – Formula 1, but he also knew he would have to be patient. But he didn't have to wait long. The beginning of the new millennium saw his career shift towards his ultimate goal. Alonso got a drive with a Minardi-backed F3000 team, but more importantly a testing contract with Minardi's F1 team. He could sense that a place in Formula 1 wasn't far away and he was right. He got his chance the following season as he was promoted to the Minardi F1 team for 2001.

WHERE IT ALL STARTED

Paired with the more experienced Tarso Marques, Alonso showed exactly what he was all about. In his first F1 outing with a back-of-the-grid race team and an uncompetitive car, he managed to outqualify Gastón Mazzacane in the Prost and Luciano Burti in the Jaguar. But, more importantly, he outqualified his new teammate by a very impressive 2.6 seconds. Alonso had shown his pedigree and though he didn't realise it at the time, he had set a pattern for the rest of the season. In the very next race in Malaysia he was outpaced in qualifying by his more experienced teammate, but showed him a clean pair of heels in the race itself as he once again finished ahead of Marques. An unreliable car saw successive DNFs, but when the two teammates did manage a finish, it was typically Alonso who was grabbing the glory by finishing in front. A change of driver saw Alex Yoong take over from Marques, but this did little to change the fortunes of Minardi or displace the undoubtedly talented Alonso, who was showing his worth, once again outpacing his teammate and grabbing an impressive 11th-place finish in his last race for Minardi in Japan.

THE GLORY YEARS

After just one season of racing with Minardi, Alonso turned down multiple offers of a seat with similar back-of-the-grid teams. So he was out in the cold with no seat for 2002. But Benetton boss Flavio Briatore – who was in charge of Alonso's career – was keen to get him into his Renault team to replace Jenson Button. While the tempting proposition of an F1 drive never materialised,

Fernando Alonso was perhaps always destined to drive an F1 car, as his kart from 1983 displays some familiar colour livery

Alonso at the Indy 500, 2019

Alonso did join Renault as a test driver. It's here that he got in over 1,640 laps in test sessions in Spain and England to hone his race skills, work with the Renault engineering team to improve his all-round racing knowledge, and get ready for the next season. Again, he was linked with a host of teams for 2003, but Briatore was no fool and promoted him alongside Jarno Trulli. In his first race he once again showed how good he was by outqualifying his teammate and grabbing a couple of points in the race. But the second race of the season in Malaysia is where fans really got to see what a talent Alonso was. He grabbed his first pole position and went on to get his first podium with a third-place finish. He was starting to show his true mettle and it wasn't long before he got his first F1 win in Hungary, neatly coupled with a pole position.

The 2004 season was another learning experience – and step towards glory – as during the offseason Alonso got involved with his engineers and the development of the latest car, the R24. His goal for the season was a simple one – improvement. He managed a pole position, four podiums and fourth place in the championship.

Alonso's momentum was building and with a car capable of taking him to the title, he was one of the preseason favourites for 2005 and he duly delivered. He got off to a blistering start with four wins, a second, a third and the only time he was off the podium was a lowly fourth at Monaco. Two DNFs put a dent in his championship hopes but he was soon back to winning ways with victories in France and Germany, and a succession of second and thirds were topped off with victory in the final race of the season in China. Alonso had done it; he was the youngest – at the time – Formula 1 world champion at the tender age of 24 years and 58 days.

With one world championship in the bag, Alonso was keen to add another and the 2006 season saw him start as one of the favourites yet again. If 2005 saw him get off to a blistering start, the beginning of the 2006 season was stratospheric. He wasn't out of the top two in the first nine races, winning six of them. A midseason wobble saw a couple of DNFs and fifth places, but Alonso brought it home in the last three races with a victory and two second places. Alonso was once again top of the pile, but this time he was the youngest two-time world champion at 25 years and 85 days.

Alonso's Benetton leads Jordan's Nick Heidfeld at the British Grand Prix, 2004

NEVER FELT AT HOME

Alonso had agreed to join McLaren back in 2005 and arrived as a two-time and reigning world champion looking to add a third successive title in 2007. McLaren had a competitive car, but Alonso was soon to discover that he had a competitive teammate in the shape of rookie Lewis Hamilton. The signs for the season were there from the off as Hamilton pulled a bold move around the outside of Alonso to get ahead of his teammate on the first lap of the first race of the new season.

Race by race the tension between Alonso, Hamilton and the team slowly started to grow. Hamilton was not happy with team orders as Alonso took first place in Monaco. Two races later at the US Grand Prix, Alonso showed his frustration when he couldn't get past Hamilton. In Hungary, Alonso blocked Hamilton in the pits to ensure he couldn't do a final qualifying lap, and at Spa he forced Hamilton off the track.

But it wasn't just on the track where the tensions were rising. Off the track, Alonso's relationship with McLaren boss Ron Dennis was at an all-time low, with Dennis revealing that they were not on speaking terms. At the end of the season, Alonso missed out on winning

Alonso celebrates his first world title in 2005 after grabbing third place in Brazil

Fernando Alonso's dream turned into a nightmare at McLaren

his third title by a single point to Kimi Räikkönen, and made it quite clear what he thought: "It is not a secret that I never really felt at home." Then, almost inevitably, McLaren announced that Alonso would be leaving and returning to his former team, Renault.

RETURN OF THE PRODIGAL SON

Alonso's short-lived reign at McLaren meant he was unexpectedly looking for a new seat for the upcoming 2008 season. He flirted with moving to Red Bull, but Benetton boss Briatore stepped into the ring with an offer that Alonso couldn't resist, and he was back with the team that brought him two world titles. But unlike previous seasons, he wasn't one of the favourites for the title. A steady rather than spectacular season saw him grab a couple of wins, a podium finish and fifth in the championship – a distant 37 points behind his old teammate Hamilton.

After declining tempting offers from Red Bull and Honda, Alonso signed a new contract with Renault, but an uncompetitive car led to a poor season by his standards with no wins, no podiums and a lowly ninth in the championship.

CLOSE, BUT NO CIGAR

Alonso was desperate to get back to winning ways and saw Ferrari as the team to make that happen. But getting there wasn't simple. A verbal agreement was to see him join in 2009, but politics got in the way. By the middle of 2009 he had made an agreement to join in 2011, but after race-fixing allegations at Renault, Alonso got his move to Ferrari in 2010 at Räikkönen's expense.

He came perilously close to that elusive third world championship in his first season, only to concede to Sebastian Vettel by a mere four points. His second season didn't live up to the first, with him finishing fourth in the championship. But it was all guns blazing for the 2012 season, with the title still in the balance heading into the last race of the season. A second place for Alonso and a sixth for Vettel once again led to heartache as the German grabbed the title by just three points. The 2013 season saw Vettel run away with the title and Alonso had to settle for second – again. His last season at Ferrari saw him team up with the man he originally replaced, Räikkönen, but Ferrari simply didn't have a car that could win and Alonso finished a disappointing sixth in the championship. His career at Ferrari came to an acrimonious end.

Alonso tried hard for glory at Ferrari

UNFINISHED BUSINESS

Alonso's first spell at McLaren had been marked with controversy and came to a bitter end. But the years had seen both McLaren team boss Dennis and Alonso mellow and mature. Dennis conceded that Alonso was one of the best, if not the best, driver in Formula 1 and wanted him back in his car. But it didn't start well. Alonso got a concussion in preseason testing and sat out the first race of the 2015 season. He then got a DNF in the second, something he was to see seven more times that season. After finishing on a pitiful 11 points, it didn't get much better in 2016. He crashed heavily in the first race and sat out the next. But a more reliable car saw Alonso get a respectable 54 points, 33 more than his teammate Button. Then in 2017 it was back to reliability issues, with

ten DNFs and Alonso threatening to leave unless Honda and McLaren could bring him a competitive car his driving talents deserved. Unfortunately they couldn't, and the inevitable finally happened.

TIME OUT

After a less than impressive second stint with McLaren, Alonso had become disillusioned with the sport, claiming it was all becoming too predictable. He decided it was time for a new adventure, stating that there were bigger challenges outside Formula 1. But what were those challenges?

The fabled Triple Crown was one mission as he tried to win the Indy 500 in 2017, 2019 and 2020, but with little success. However, the famous 24 Hours of Le Mans was a more fruitful race ground, as he won twice in 2018 and 2019 with Toyota. But other motorsports couldn't provide the challenge he was looking for and in 2020 he decided it was time to get back to his first love – Formula 1.

THIRD TIME LUCKY

At the age of 39 Alonso was back in the F1 game, he was back in the sport he loved and the lure of a third stint with his favourite F1 family (Renault) for the 2021 season was simply too hard to resist. The team were committed to Formula 1 and getting back to the top of the F1 tree with Alpine and Alonso at the wheel. But two seasons were not quite the triumphant return Alonso would have wanted. So partway through the 2022 season Alonso announced he was replacing the retiring Sebastian Vettel at Aston Martin. He still feels he deserves a seat in Formula 1, and talent doesn't just disappear – so this double world champion will always be welcome.

Alonso driving for Aston Martin in 2024

Protests, blackmail and fines

Fernando Alonso is not a man to avoid controversy, as demonstrated by the blocking of his teammate during qualifying for the 2007 Hungarian Grand Prix. Lewis Hamilton was meant to let Alonso pass on the track but decided not to, so he took matters into his own hands with unsubtle time-wasting behaviour as the two stacked in the pits. Hamilton didn't get back out for a second qualifying lap, meaning Alonso took pole. But not for long. After a protest from Hamilton's team, Alonso was handed a five-place grid penalty.

Alonso was not a happy man and this led to perhaps the biggest controversy of his career. The next morning, a few hours before the race, Alonso demanded a meeting with team boss Ron Dennis to 'discuss' the previous day's proceedings. Alonso threatened Dennis that if the team did not do what he wanted, he would reveal to the FIA emails he had that were relevant to the 'spygate' case. This is where chief designer Mike Coughlan was found in possession of a 780-page document of Ferrari intellectual property. Alonso insisted that McLaren make Hamilton run out of fuel in the race. Dennis and his second in command, Martin Whitmarsh, didn't like being blackmailed and phoned FIA president Max Mosley. It is believed that it was this phone call that led to McLaren being excluded from the Constructors' Championship, receiving a $100 million fine and Alonso negotiating his way out of his contract.

Battle of the giants. Alonso teamed up with Hamilton for a single, tension-filled season at McLaren in 2007

Legendary DRIVERS

SEBASTIAN VETTEL

THE CHARGING BULL

Sebastian Vettel smashed countless Formula 1 records but couldn't find the finesse at Ferrari

It is said that if you want to build a champion, then you need to start young. This is certainly true of Sebastian Vettel, the man who spent the first half of his Formula 1 career becoming the youngest driver to achieve a whole host of records. Born in Heppenheim, Germany, Vettel's karting career started by the age of three, thanks in no small part to his motorsport-obsessed father Norbert. He was driving competitively by seven and impressed instantly with his skill, fearlessness and fascination with the technical side of the sport. It was this blend of dedication and ability that saw young Vettel rack up multiple wins and trophies, one of which was handed to him by none other than F1 legend and Vettel's personal hero Michael Schumacher. Clearly this was a child destined for greatness.

Long before Red Bull were an active Formula 1 team, they sponsored promising young drivers to help them progress through the motorsport world. Vettel was one of those drivers and, aged 13, was signed up to the Red Bull Junior Team. That clearly helped as Vettel stormed to the 2004 Formula BMW ADAC title, winning 18 of the 20 races. This form attracted the attention of Sauber, for whom Vettel test drove while still a teenager. Then, in 2007, he stood in for Robert Kubica at the United States Grand Prix and drove a masterful race at Indianapolis. Vettel qualified seventh and ended the race eighth. That earned him a debut point, becoming the youngest driver to do so. This clearly impressed Toro Rosso, who were effectively Red Bull's feeder team. Four races later they parachuted the young German into a seat where he struggled initially, finishing near the back of the field in his first four races and recording two consecutive DNFs, before a stunning drive in China saw him finish fourth. He did enough in that half-season to retain his seat the following year and repaid Toro Rosso handsomely. Despite recording four DNFs at the start of the 2008 season, Vettel stunned the world of motorsport by claiming pole at the Italian Grand Prix at Monza and, despite soaking wet conditions, cruising to a dominant win. It was Toro Rosso's first Grand Prix victory and made Vettel both the youngest-ever polesitter and youngest-ever winner in the sport. Vettel was suddenly hot property indeed.

His performances in a car that could usually be found near the back of the grid convinced the main Red Bull team to take a punt on him after he outscored veterans Mark Webber and David Coulthard, despite driving the inferior car. He replaced the retiring Coulthard to partner Webber in the exciting Red Bull garage, and what a decision that was.

Red Bull had been mixing it in the midfield since they bought out Jaguar in 2005, but their new star catapulted them to the front of the grid. Vettel's victory in China was the team's first in Formula 1 and he followed it up with wins in Great Britain, Japan and Abu Dhabi. These helped him finish second in the driver standings, 11 points behind surprise champion Jenson Button. Clearly Red Bull and Vettel were a perfect match for each other. The 2010 season saw a major shake-up in the sport with 25 points now given to the race winner to try to encourage drivers to push for the victory, rather than settle for a safe second. This suited the fast and ultra-competitive Vettel down to the ground, as he won in Malaysia and Europe. It was a five-way battle for the title for much of the season as Vettel and Webber took on Ferrari's two-time champion Fernando Alonso, as well as McLaren's British duo of Button and Lewis Hamilton. It looked like Alonso was going to take his third crown with victory in South Korea, but Vettel won in Brazil to keep the championship

Say I'm you're number one. He most certainly was, for four years on the trot

Vettel driving for Toro Rosso (right) tussles with Rubens Barrichello of Honda (front) and McLaren's Heikki Kovalainen, Canada 2008

alive. Going into the final race in Abu Dhabi, Alonso had an eight-point lead over Webber and a 15-point lead over Vettel, with Hamilton needing an incredible set of results to win the title. Vettel did all he could, leading from pole and cruising to a dominant victory and ending Hamilton's chances of a second title – but what about the men who could deny him a maiden championship? He faced a nervous wait after crossing the line but, with Alonso and Webber finishing seventh and eighth respectively, Vettel was confirmed as the youngest-ever Formula 1 world champion. Remarkably it was the first time he had led the championship all season and he had done it at the age of 23, beating the mark set by Hamilton two years earlier. Vettel was already a history-making superstar, having defeated a brilliant two-time champion and an experienced teammate to the coveted title – an amazing achievement.

However, he wasn't done there, not by a long shot. Vettel enjoyed a staggeringly dominant season in 2011. He won five of the first six races of the season and then five of the final eight, claiming a second title with an incredible four races still to go – the joint third-fastest win in history. He also became the youngest two-time champion, taking the record off Alonso.

Like Alonso, it looked like Vettel would get stuck on two championships, after a poor start to the 2012 season. He won just one of the opening 13 races of the season, trailed Alonso by a whopping 39 points and was also behind Hamilton and Kimi Räikkönen in the standings. The turning point came in Singapore where he roared to victory, the first of four in a row that catapulted him to the top of the standings. The championship went down to the final race of the season again, but this time it was a straight fight between just Vettel and Alonso. Vettel started fourth with Alonso in seventh at a wet Interlagos, but it was the worst possible start for the German as he lost places off the line and was then involved in a collision with Bruno Senna, spinning and falling dead last. Undeterred, Vettel fought his way back up the field and was running eighth before too long. Alonso put in a supreme display in awful conditions to get himself into second, but needed Vettel to finish eighth or lower to take the title. It wasn't to be, however, as Vettel squeezed past compatriot and hero Schumacher into sixth and when Paul di Resta's crash brought out the safety car, Vettel just needed to cross the line to become a three-time champion. Aged just 25 he became the youngest triple champion, reaching the

Sebastian Vettel taming the Red Bull

Vettel and Schumacher had a long, special relationship – even as the former was stealing the latter's records

mark six years quicker than Ayrton Senna. In winning his third title in a row, Vettel had also taken another age-related record off the man who had inspired him as a youngster, achieving the three-peat eight years quicker than the great Schumacher.

So after three consecutive championship wins, could Vettel make it a fourth? He controversially won in Malaysia after disobeying team orders to stay behind teammate Mark Webber when the Red Bull duo were running first and second, before wins at Bahrain, Canada and Germany saw him take a 38-point lead over Räikkönen at the summer break. If any of his rivals thought there was a chink in his armour then they were to be sadly mistaken, as in the end it was no contest. Vettel went on an unprecedented nine-race winning streak, taking every single remaining Grand Prix of the season in an unheard-of display of dominance, speed and consistency. From a potentially treacherous position, Vettel had blown away the pack and cantered to the title with three races to spare. That made it four wins on the spin for Vettel, putting him level with Alain Prost and only behind Juan Manuel Fangio and Schumacher. Once again, Vettel was the youngest to four titles by some distance and looked well on his way to matching Schumacher's record of five straight championship titles. However, while no other driver could match his peerless talent, something else got in his way. In a bid to become greener, Formula 1 bosses insisted engines be replaced by hybrid power units, which played right into the hands of the Mercedes team of Hamilton and Nico Rosberg. The pair won 16 of the 19 races, ending Red Bull's stranglehold on the championship and Vettel's four-year reign as champion. The only non-Mercedes driver to win a race was a Red Bull driver, but it wasn't the four-time champion. Webber had retired, leaving a space for his fellow Australian Daniel Ricciardo. The ever-smiling, popular and quick Ricciardo won in Canada, Hungary and Belgium, finishing third in the driver standings, two

Vettel showed what he was made of to take the 2012 title

places above Vettel who failed to win a single race and made the podium just four times.

Vettel wasn't used to not winning. 2014 was just the second time in his career, and the first since his rookie season, in which he'd failed to take the chequered flag. He was unhappy at Red Bull, who had failed to give him a car in which he felt comfortable, and the emergence of exciting young talent Ricciardo mimicked Vettel's own blockbuster entrance to F1 where he usurped established team leader Webber. This prompted him to shock the world of motorsport and seek a new challenge away from the team that had delivered him four consecutive world titles. He found it in the form of the most glamorous team in F1. Ferrari and Alonso had had a fractious relationship, with Scuderia unable to provide a car worthy of the two-time champion's talents. Alonso and Ferrari parted ways and in slid Vettel to the Prancing Horse's stable, looking to emulate his idol Schumacher. Things looked promising, with Vettel winning the second race of the season in Malaysia, but once again the field was blown away by the dominance of Mercedes. Vettel was well behind the duo of Hamilton and Rosberg, but miles ahead of the rest of the field and the partnership with Ferrari showed promising signs. However, the 2016 season was a disaster. Vettel failed to win a race for the second time in three seasons, with driver errors and team failures costing him several opportunities to take a Grand Prix. To make matters worse, he finished behind the Red Bull of Ricciardo and just about edged out young upstart Max Verstappen, a teenager who would eventually take some of Vettel's records.

Things had to get better and in 2017 they did. He won two of the first three races of the season after Ferrari delivered a car many considered to be the best on the grid. His running battle with Hamilton was one for the ages, the championship lead swapping on a regular basis. The pair clashed more than once, banging wheels in Spain before another incident in Azerbaijan. With the race behind a safety car, Vettel ran into Hamilton from behind, then drew alongside him and swerved into the Brit. Vettel initially blamed Hamilton for the incident, before taking responsibility. More engine problems and collisions for Vettel meant that Hamilton won the title with a couple of races to spare, but he was left with a sense of what might have been were it not for reliability issues and his own temper.

A move to Ferrari was the next challenge for Vettel. The Prancing Horse initially seemed like a good fit, but ultimately didn't lead to further title success

That was to prove to be the closest Vettel got to a title in the red of Ferrari. He wasn't able to mount any kind of challenge to Hamilton the following season, despite again having one of the best cars on the grid. The following two seasons were disasters, finishing behind yet another young, exciting new teammate in Charles Leclerc. Just as he had done at Red Bull, with an uncompetitive car and a new kid on the block, Vettel moved teams, this time to Aston Martin. He and teammate Lance Stroll were perennial midfielders, but Vettel did manage two podiums. He should have earned a maiden win for his new team in Hungary after a superb drive, but devastatingly had insufficient fuel left at the end of the race for testing and was disqualified.

There will always be question marks around Vettel's career. Is he an all-time great, or did he just happen to be in the right car at the right time? It can certainly be argued that every time he has been challenged, either by a rival or a teammate, he has appeared to come up short and jumped ship. Often, in the heat of battle, he came off second best and it was only when he was leading pole to flag that he shone. However, it cannot be denied that as a leader, as a driver and as a competitor he is right up there with the best. No one breaks the records of Alonso, Senna and Schumacher without being an exceptionally talented driver. While it is true that he might have been in the right place at the right time, Vettel sure made his time in the hot seat count.

Vettel in an Aston Martin at the British Grand Prix, 2021

The Raging Bull

As the likes of Schumacher, Hamilton and Verstappen have shown, you need a bit of fire in your belly if you are to achieve greatness in Formula 1. Vettel is no exception and has had a number of notable moments when his will to win took him over the edge. The first sign of this attitude was in 2010 when he tried to overtake teammate Webber and caused a dramatic crash that cost Red Bull victory and knocked him out of the race.

If that wasn't bad enough, in 2013 Webber was leading from Vettel at the Malaysian Grand Prix. Despite team orders telling the pair to hold their positions to guarantee the 1-2, Vettel repeatedly attacked, at one point being told by team principal Christian Horner, "This is silly, Seb. Come on". The German eventually got past and won the race, but ruined his professional relationship with Webber and had to apologise to the furious Australian. Then at Ferrari there was that bizarre incident with Hamilton where he bashed into his rival twice, before another astonishing moment at the 2019 Canadian Grand Prix. Vettel was leading but, under pressure from Hamilton, went onto the grass. In returning to the track he squeezed Hamilton against the wall, which the stewards ruled deserved a five-second penalty. Vettel won the race, but the penalty dropped him to second. Furious at the decision, he swapped over the first and second-placed boards in the winners enclosure to make his feelings clear. Never one to shirk a challenge or a fight, Vettel truly has the mentality of a champion.

Vettel leaving no one in any doubt who he thought the real race winner was in Canada in 2019

As the 67th instalment of the World Championship reared into view in 2016, the odds on Lewis Hamilton becoming only the fourth driver ever to claim a hat-trick of consecutive F1 crowns were short. Team-mate Nico Rosberg, however, was to unexpectedly emerge as the dominant force to extend the era of Anglo-German Grand Prix dominance

FORMULA ONE SURGES ON 2016-24

2016 was Nico Rosberg's year, but he was plagued with brake issues at the Monaco Grand Prix and reluctantly let teammate Lewis Hamilton pass him in the race

Victory in 2015 had elevated Lewis Hamilton into rarefied motorsport company. He now proudly stood alongside the legendary names of Fangio, Brabham, Stewart, Lauda, Piquet, Senna, Prost, Schumacher and Vettel as a three-time world champion, and with Mercedes in no mood to relinquish their pre-eminent position in the battle of the constructors, not least to perennial rivals Ferrari, the received wisdom ahead of the new season was the British star who would once again emerge as the leader of the pack.

The campaign would be an unprecedentedly arduous one. The return of both the German and European Grands Prix saw the calendar expand to a record 21 races and when the cars lined up on the grid in March for the start of the Australian Grand Prix on the streets of Melbourne, Hamilton's pole position seemed to confirm all the pre-season predictions. Rosberg had not read the same script though and a poor start from the defending champion was all the invitation the German needed as he took control of proceedings Down Under, overhauled Sebastain Vettel on the 35th lap when the Ferrari pitted, and cantered untroubled to the chequered flag.

Any thoughts Rosberg's triumph in Australia was an anomaly were quickly dispelled with victory in the next three races in Bahrain, China and Russia. Hamilton's uncharacteristic early struggles finally came to an end in Monaco in May when he successfully fended off the challenge of Red Bull's Daniel Ricciardo in the initially wet conditions to secure his first victory of the season. Rosberg limped home in seventh, a result saw his lead at the top of the championship table reduced to 24 points.

The remainder of the campaign saw the Mercedes pair jostle almost exclusively for the crown. Six wins in seven in Europe for Hamilton over the summer dragged the Brit conclusively back into contention before Rosberg replied with maximum points in Belgium, Italy and Singapore to set up a grandstand finish to the year's fluctuating rivalry.

The climax came over 55 laps of the Yas Marina Circuit in Abu Dhabi at the end of November. Rosberg was defending a precarious 12-point lead in the standings, meaning a win for Hamilton and third-place finish or worse for the German would dramatically hand the title to his team-mate. The Brit secured pole

Hamilton and Rosberg were originally friends from their karting days. This was torn to shreds once the duo both became title contenders for Mercedes

Crowned World Champion in 2016, Rosberg celebrates with his Mercedes team flying the German flag

to intensify the expectation and never surrendered first place in the race itself and it was all about whether Rosberg could come safely in second.

Despite repeated team orders over the Mercedes radio to speed up, Hamilton stubbornly slowed down in an attempt to bunch up the field and give Vettel and Red Bull's Max Verstappen the opportunity to reel in Rosberg but the German successfully fended off the challenge which lingered in his rear-view mirror. He finished less than half a second adrift of Hamilton but second on this occasion felt like first as he became the second German driver to reach the summit of Formula One after Michael Schumacher. His title success also saw Rosberg become part of only the second father-and-son duo to claim the title, following in his father Keke's famous footsteps and 1982 championship triumph.

Hopes of another iconic duel between Rosberg and Hamilton in 2017 were abruptly dashed just five days after the former's career-defining moment in Abu Dhabi. At the FIA Awards ceremony in Vienna, the victorious German announced his immediate retirement from the sport at the age of 31 and was replaced at Mercedes by Finn Valtteri Bottas. For the first time since 1994, when Alain Prost walked away from Formula One after winning the title, an edition of the Championship would not feature the reigning champion on the grid.

If the 2016 fight for the driver's title had been a largely private Mercedes party, 2017 was a public showdown between the German giants and Ferrari in the shape of Vettel, eager to reclaim his F1 crown three seasons after last lifting the trophy. The four-time former champion made all the early running, igniting his campaign with victory in the opening race in Australia for his first maximum points haul since September 2015, a significant result which underlined the belief the days of an unchallenged Mercedes procession were over.

Eight podium finishes, including four victories, in the opening 11 races gave Vettel a double digit but not decisive lead over Hamilton by August, but with the winning line almost in sight, the Ferrari star's season imploded. A race-ending crash over which he had no control in Singapore in September, coupled with Hamilton's 60th career Grand Prix triumph, was pivotal and when the German again failed to finish in Japan

Mercedes recruited ex-Williams driver Valtteri Bottas to replace Rosberg in 2017

at the Suzuka circuit due to a catastrophic spark plug failure, the writing was on the wall. In stark contrast, Hamilton found enhanced speed and consistency as his principal rival faded, and he was anointed world champion for a fourth time, with two races to spare, in Mexico in late October despite only limping home in ninth. His emotional victory gave Hamilton the standalone distinction as the most successful Formula One driver in the already decorated history of British motorsport, eclipsing three-time champion Jackie Stewart, while for Mercedes it was the fourth year running in which they had left the competition in their wake in the Constructors' Championship.

THE HAMILTON ERA

Although the years following the double tragedy of the deaths of Ayrton Senna and Roland Ratzenberger in San Marino in 1994, had mercifully seen only one further F1 fatality when Frenchman Jules Bianchi lost his life prematurely racing during the Japanese Grand Prix, the 2018 season nonetheless welcomed another new safety feature with the introduction of the 'halo', a state-of-the-art cockpit crash protection device. The development attracted aesthetically focused criticism in some quarters of the paddock, but the device won over its doubters in August at the Spa-Francorchamps. When the McLaren of Fernando Alonso was sent airborne on the opening lap after a shunt from behind, F1 debutant Charles Leclerc's Sauber found itself in the firing line only for the 20-year-old's wishbone-shaped halo to absorb the brunt of a potentially fatal collision and avert a head-on impact. After the race, Leclerc conceded he had been lucky to have escaped serious injury or worse.

Free to enjoy the thrills and spills of the 2018

The number 44 of Hamilton leads Sebastian Vettel during the United States Grand Prix, Austin Texas 2017

Lewis Hamilton beats polesitter Bottas, ahead of Ferrari's Kimi Räikkönen and Max Verstappen's Red Bull at the Austrian Grand Prix, 2018. Unusually both Mercedes cars later retired from the race

LEFT TO RIGHT: Jules Bianchi who lost his life at the Japanese Grand Prix in 2014

The much lauded 'halo', first used in the 2018 F1 season

season with driver safety further assured, F1 fans were mesmerised by another titanic tussle for the title and, from the perspective of Hamilton supporters, it was another unforgettable year. As it had over the previous 12 months, the campaign played out as a two-horse race between the British serial winner and Vettel and although the championship lead changed five times over the course of the season, Hamilton emerged as the victor to equal the iconic Argentinian Juan Manuel Fangio's milestone, set back in the 1950s, of a remarkable five Formula One crowns. The campaign was the first in the sport's history that two four-time champions had raced against each other, prompting the media to dub the head-to-head as the 'Fight for Five'.

The season-opening Australian Grand Prix saw Vettel draw first blood courtesy of the timely deployment of the virtual safety car after the front left tyre on Romain Grosjean's Haas became problematic. Hamilton had to wait until April and Azerbaijan until he was celebrating on top of the podium but at the half point of the year, following the German's second career victory at Silverstone, Vettel had built a slender eight-point lead in the Driver's Championship.

The deficit sparked an irresistible surge in form for Hamilton. In the closing 11 races he claimed victory eight times, including four on the bounce in Italy, Singapore, Russia and Japan, while his worst finish was fourth in

the penultimate in Mexico in October. The Red Bull duo of Ricciardo and Verstappen locked out the front row on the grid at the Autódromo Hermanos Rodríguez, with the latter eventually taking the chequered flag, and although Vettel improved his fourth in qualifying into second in the race itself, Hamilton's 12-point return was enough to secure the title. Two season-ending wins in Brazil and Abu Dhabi were the icing on the cake and Hamilton was crowned champion by what was ultimately resounding 88 points ahead of Vettel, while Ferrari's second driver Kimi Räikkönen was third.

Marking the final championship of the decade, the 2019 season saw the FIA continue to alter the format and brought in a bonus point system for the driver – and constructor – posting the fastest lap in each of the year's 21 races. It was the first time since 1959 the additional, if minimal, reward had been on offer.

Surprisingly, 2019 saw the Ferrari challenge to Mercedes recede with the Prancing Horse duo of Leclerc and Vettel registering just three victories between them all year and the mantle of challenger-in-chief to Hamilton fell to team-mate Bottas and, to a lesser extent, Verstappen in his improving Red Bull. In truth however, Hamilton's charge to a sixth title was irresistible from early on and his dominance was underlined by the fact he was confirmed as the sport's pre-eminent racer with two events to spare.

Despite the lack of real jeopardy as the season unfolded, there were still two memorable weekends that further burnished Hamilton's already storied CV. The first came at the Chinese Grand Prix in April. It was only the 16th staging of the race at Shanghai International Circuit but it was nonetheless a historic event, the 1,000th officially recognised Grand Prix race. Starting on pole, Hamilton lead throughout in China for what was a fitting triumph for arguably the sport's greatest ever driver on such a significant anniversary.

If his success in China was one for the record books, the result at the British Grand Prix in the summer was all about emotions. Already safely ensconced at the top of the driver standings, Hamilton prepared for his home race level on five career victories at Silverstone

Leap of faith. Lewis Hamilton jumps out of his Mercedes at the sheer delight of setting pole position at the 2019 British Grand Prix

Ferrari rising star Charles Leclerc leads the 2019 Italian Grand Prix ahead of the two Mercedes of Hamilton and Bottas. Leclerc went on to win the race to the delight of the tifosi

alongside compatriot Jim Clark and Prost. It proved to be a dramatic race with Vettel and Verstappen crashing on lap 36, both cars spinning into the gravel, but up ahead Hamilton had already taken full advantage of a safety car on lap 16 to pit after Antonio Giovinazzi's Alfa Romeo suffered a mechanical failure and still emerge ahead of Bottas and the result was effectively sealed with 36 laps yet to complete.

In his irresistible march to an unrivalled sixth British GP triumph, Hamilton also set a new Silverstone lap record of 1:27.369, further cementing his enduring love affair with the iconic track.

Confirmation of his sixth F1 crown came in Texas at the United States Grand Prix. Bottas began the race with a vanishingly remote chance of overhauling his stablemate and won at the Circuit of the Americas, his fourth victory of the season, but it spoke volumes about Hamilton's relentlessly competitive nature that he pursued the Finn with a ferocity that belied his commanding championship lead even though the champagne was already on ice. Tantalisingly, his title win left Hamilton just one behind Schumacher's once seemingly insurmountable tally of seven F1 crowns.

There was double cause for celebration in the Mercedes camp in 2019 as the German team wrapped up their sixth consecutive Constructors' Championship success, equalling Ferrari's proud record of sequential victories set between 1999 and 2004.

SEVENTH HEAVEN

Originally slated to begin in March, the 2020 Championship, the 70th anniversary of the inaugural Formula One season of 1950, was delayed due to the ravages of COVID-19 and it

A relaxed Lewis Hamilton was cleaning up World Championships

was not until July that the teams were finally able to do battle again. In an inevitably truncated calendar of 17 races the Austrian Grand Prix in Styria marked F1's rebirth, albeit behind closed doors at the Red Bull Ring, and it was a thrilling return to the sporting fray in which Bottas masterfully nursed his temperamental Mercedes around to take maximum points.

A collision with Red Bull's Alex Albon cost Hamilton with 11 laps remaining, which sent the Thai spinning into the gravel, cost the defending champion a five-second penalty and ultimately a place on the podium but it was a rare error in what was otherwise to be a majestic year in which the 35-year-old which ensured the keepers of the sport's record books were kept busy.

Six wins in the next nine races following his Austrian disappointment put Hamilton firmly in control of the

Not even a global pandemic could prevent the force of Mercedes and Hamilton race wins in 2020

title race, but it was at the one-off Eifel Grand Prix at the Nürburgring in October, the first Grand Prix at the legendary German track since 2013, that he etched his name yet again into motorsport history. Starting second on the grid, Hamilton took a lead he never relinquished when Bottas locked up on the first turn of lap 13 and stormed to the chequered flag for a second win at the Nürburgring after his 2011 triumph with McLaren.

Far more significantly, the result gave the Brit the 91st Grand Prix victory of his already glittering career and in doing so he equalled the milestone of chequered flags set by Schumacher. The German icon's final win had come at the Chinese Grand Prix in 2006 and with six races of the 2020 campaign still to be contested, it was merely a matter of time before Hamilton ascended to the top of the all-time standings in glorious isolation.

Unsurprisingly he took the opportunity to make history at the first time of asking at the Portuguese Grand Prix two weeks later. A cold track at the Algarve International Circuit and an early sprinkling of rain saw Hamilton initially struggle, slipping down to third behind Bottas and McLaren's Carlos Sainz Jr., but once his tyres had warmed up, there was a familiar sense of inevitability as he chased down Bottas again. He passed the Finn on lap 20 and the remainder of proceedings afforded the socially distanced crowd ample opportunity to salute the most prolific driver Formula One has ever seen. It was a mere footnote that his unprecedented 92nd victory – his first had come at the Canadian Grand Prix 13 years earlier – extended his Championship lead to a massive 77 points.

His irresistible coronation as world champion was confirmed the following month at the Turkish Grand Prix. Rain in Istanbul made it a chaotic weekend of racing, as Racing Point's Lance Stroll claimed a shock, maiden pole position after qualifying, while Hamilton finished off the pace in sixth, but once the lights went out 24 hours later, the Mercedes star was characteristically brilliant. He took full advantage of the team's decision to opt for a one-stop strategy in Turkey and by the end

Lance Stroll of Racing Point claimed his first pole position at the Turkish Grand Prix, 2020

Max Verstappen got the better of Lewis Hamilton at the United States Grand Prix in 2021

of the race was a decisive 31 seconds clear of second-placed Sergio Pérez in his Racing Point. His 94th career triumph confirmed Hamilton as a seven-time Formula One champion alongside Schumacher. "I remember watching Michael winning the championships," he said. "Just to get one, or two, or three, it's so hard to get. Seven is just unimaginable."

The inevitable debate about the greatest of the pair soon followed. At the age of 35 and in his 14th F1 season, Hamilton was at exactly the same stage of his career in terms of age and experience when the German had found himself in seventh heaven back in 2004, but although the Brit had equalled rather than eclipsed Schumacher's haul of titles in 2020, he had already comfortably surpassed many of his rival's other major records, including most Formula One wins, pole positions and podium finishes. The German was 43 when he had raced for the final time in Brazil in 2012, suggesting realistically that Hamilton had the best part of another decade in which to win an eighth title and end any increasingly lingering doubt in the greatest ever debate.

Bottas gives a congratulatory fist bump to Hamilton on his pole at the British Grand Prix, 2021

DUTCH MASTER

Before Max Verstappen's Formula One bow for Toro Rosso at the 2015 Australian Grand Prix, a maiden F1 entry in which he had been forced to retire, the Netherlands had produced 15 Formula One drivers who had failed to win a single race between them in 263 combined attempts between 1952 and 1986. One of his predecessors, father Jos, had registered two podiums in his 107 entries, but it was the younger Verstappen who finally ended the nation's long wait for victory when he had taken the chequered flag for Red Bull in Spain in 2016.

The intervening years had seen the Dutch driver make solid but not pyrotechnic progress up the F1 pecking order. Nine maximum-point hauls between 2017 and 2020, as well as back-to-back third-place finishes in the Drivers' Championship, were signallers that Verstappen was becoming a genuine force to be reckoned with, and with Red Bull continuing to grow in strength, 16 years after the team's formation, 2020 gave way to 2021 with

the 23-year-old well positioned to dethrone Hamilton and end his four-year reign as top dog.

Few however could have predicted the sheer drama – and controversy – the climax of a thrilling season brought. The battle between Verstappen and Hamilton was truly titanic, the pair claiming victory in 17 of the 21 races that preceded the season finale in Abu Dhabi a fortnight before Christmas, and as a result of the gladiatorial nature of their rivalry, they collided no less than three times (at the British, Hungarian and Italian GPs) with both pushing each other to the limit as the championship lead changed hands multiple times.

The mouth-watering outcome was that the rivals arrived at the Yas Marina Circuit in the United Arab Emirates in December improbably level on points. Hamilton made the stronger start in Abu Dhabi and as the race neared its denouement, the champion was in front and seemingly on course for a historic eighth title. The F1 gods, however, had other ideas and when Nicholas Latifi crashed his Williams with only five laps remaining, the picture suddenly changed.

The deployment of the safety car was the only thing that followed that was standard. Mercedes decided not to pit their driver for fresh tyres, fearing Verstappen would not follow suit and inherit the lead without a fight. Red Bull did though opt for new rubber, but with five lapped cars – those of Lando Norris, Fernando Alonso, Esteban Ocon, Leclerc and Vettel – between the

Desert storm. Ready to pounce on the World Champion, Hamilton sees the young pretender to the throne Max Verstappen in his mirrors with a new set of tyres, at the Abu Dhabi Grand Prix, 2021

two title protagonists, Mercedes were confident there was sufficient traffic between the drivers to preserve Hamilton's advantage. Protocol dictated the lapped cars would retain their track position, but after a complaint from Red Bull, race director Michael Masi ordered the quintet to overtake Hamilton. The contentious edict cleared the way for Verstappen who, benefitting from his new tyres, sped past the Brit on turn five of the final lap and took the chequered flag.

Celebrations in the Red Bull camp were nonetheless delayed. Two unsuccessful Mercedes appeals against Masi's pivotal intervention took four hours to be dismissed and late on a day of undiluted drama, Verstappen was finally confirmed as the new Formula One champion.

Such was the box office nature of the conclusion of one of the greatest seasons in F1 history, many of the year's significant milestones were lost in the noise. Verstappen's triumph made him, at the age of 23 years and 134 days, the youngest world champion ever and the first for Red Bull since Vettel eight years earlier. He also became the first Honda-powered driver to lift the trophy since Senna in 1991, and the first not to hail from the UK or Germany to take the coveted crown since Finland's Kimi Räikkönen in 2007.

Verstappen was eventually able to celebrate winning the 2021 World Championship for Red Bull

There were though two significant crumbs of comfort for Hamilton and Mercedes despite their Abu Dhabi heartbreak. The Russian Grand Prix in September saw Hamilton become the sport's only driver to register a century of Formula One victories while the star's second-place finish in the UAE, coupled with Bottas's sixth, was enough for the German team to secure a record-extending eighth consecutive Constructors' Championship title.

Whether the young Dutch driver could cope with the pressure of his status as reigning champion, rather than being merely a potential usurper, was the question on the lips of F1 fans as the new season loomed in 2022 but the mettle of his title defence was taken out of his hands in Bahrain in late March. Verstappen's Red Bull suffered a fuel system failure late on in the season opener in Sakhir, forcing him to reluctantly retire and leaving Leclerc to seal victory from pole.

Max, now with number 1 on his car stalks Red Bull teammate Sergio "Checo" Pérez, 2022

It was not the bow as champion driver or team had hoped for, but Verstappen wasted no time in reaffirming his credentials seven days later in Saudi Arabia. From fourth on the grid, he edged out Leclerc by less than a second in Jeddah for the win and with his first points of the year on the board, Verstappen never looked back. Tellingly Hamilton, who was starting his 180th race with Mercedes to set yet another F1 record for the most drives for a single team, only finished 10th in Saudi Arabia. It was a result which hinted at a change, whether permanent or not, in the sport's power dynamic with Leclerc and Verstappen's team-mate Pérez now the principal threat to the Dutchman's title aspirations.

In truth, the challenge was never more than fleeting. A sequence of three successive wins at the Emilia Romagna, Miami and Spanish Grands Prix through April and May underlined Verstappen was the man to beat and he hammered home the message between July and September with five back-to-back wins during the European leg of the calendar. With four races still to be contested, Verstappen was crowned champion for a second time in early October in Japan when he was triumphant for the 12th time in the year at the Suzuka International circuit. It was a race scheduled for 53 laps that ultimately lasted just 28 due to heavy rain and a first-lap crash for Sainz, but the truncated nature of events did nothing to detract from Verstappen's achievement as he became the tenth driver to successfully defend the title.

The Red Bull star eventually finished a massive 146 points clear of Leclerc in the final standings. Overall he claimed 15 victories in 22 attempts, including nine in the closing 11 weekends, while his total tally of 454 points surpassed the previous season-best of 413 set by Hamilton three years earlier.

If 2022 was comprehensive confirmation of Verstappen's ascension as top dog, it was also a pivotal season in the battle of the constructors. Fuelled by the Dutchman's brilliance, Red Bull claimed the Championship for the first time since 2013 ahead of Ferrari in a very distant second. In contrast the previously all-conquering Mercedes, who struggled to come to terms with the FIA's latest raft of regulations, registered a solitary win all year. It was George Russell rather than Hamilton who took the chequered flag in

George Russell takes home his first victory for Mercedes at the Brazilian Grand Prix, 2022

the São Paulo Grand Prix for their only success while his team-mate endured the first ever winless season of his 15-year-long career – he also failed to claim pole for the first time – as Mercedes found themselves in the unfamiliar position of out of sight in third in the Constructors' Championship table.

RED BULL RAMPANT

To describe 2023 as the year in which Verstappen elevated himself from F1 star and double world champion to the next level, a bona fide all-time Grand Prix legend to be discussed in the same reverential breath as the sport's true elite, would be an understatement. The mercurial 26-year-old seemed to be racing on a different plane to the mere mortals he shared the track with and stormed to his hat-trick of titles in devastating style.

Victory in the opening race of the season in Bahrain came as no surprise as Verstappen and Red Bull hinted at the utter dominance that was to unfold over the following nine months. The champion led from the first to 57th and final lap, and it spoke volumes about the serenity of his win that the focus quickly switched from his procession at the front to Fernando Alonso's valiant day's work in his Aston Martin, the Spaniard initially dropping down from fifth on the grid on the opening lap behind Hamilton and Russell only to entertainingly weave his way back up the field and claim the third and final place on the podium.

Fellow Red Bull driver Pérez gave what proved to be a false early impression that the season might be a contest with his wins in Saudi Arabia and Azerbaijan, but from that point onwards, beginning with the Miami Grand Prix in early May, Verstappen was untouchable.

Verstappen speeds off at the 2023 Austrian Grand Prix, ahead of the two Ferrari's of Leclerc and Sainz, with Hamilton and the McLaren of Norris behind

His triumph in Florida was a psychological hammer blow to Pérez's title hopes. The Mexican had qualified on pole while Verstappen started back in ninth after Leclerc crashed in second qualifying, leaving the champion frustratingly unable to set a time, but the apparently insurmountable gap between the two Red Bulls as the lights went out was a mirage. He overhauled his team-mate as early as lap 19 when Perez pitted for medium tyres and the race was over.

His Miami masterclass was the catalyst for the greatest winning sequence from any driver in F1 history. Success in the United States was followed by wins in Monaco, Spain, Canada and Austria as Verstappen decimated the rest of the field, and in July he claimed his first career victory at the British Grand Prix, outpacing Lando Norris in his McLaren and the Mercedes of Hamilton at Silverstone. Six consecutive triumphs became seven in Hungary a fortnight later but the Dutchman's relentless form did not falter as he won the Belgian Grand Prix at the Spa-Francorchamps.

The ninth leg of his record-breaking run came in his home race, the Dutch GP at the Circuit Zandvoort, watched by over 300,000 unashamedly partisan fans over the late August weekend. Verstappen had been king of the Zandvoort track in both 2021 and 2022 and completed his home hat-trick in characteristically emphatic style, recovering from briefly surrendering his lead from pole to Pérez in wet conditions only to recapture first place on lap 13. A red flag and 45-minute delay with eight laps remaining failed to derail his charge and he took the chequered flag almost four seconds clear of Alonso.

Victory saw Verstappen become only the second driver after Britain's Jim Clark between 1963 and 1965 to win three Dutch Grands Prix in a row. More significantly his triumph, his ninth in succession, equalled Sebastian Vettel's record for Formula One's longest winning sequence which the four-time German champion had set a decade earlier.

The European leg of F1's 2023 global adventure concluded with the Italian Grand Prix at Monza seven days later. Surprisingly Verstappen was forced to concede pole to Carlos Sainz and his Ferrari, the Spaniard going just 0.013 seconds quicker in qualifying, but it was a minor setback that the runaway Championship leader brushed off with typical aplomb. Sainz successfully fended off Verstappen for 14 laps in Italy, but the pressure of his rival in his rear-view mirror eventually took its toll and the Spaniard locked his brakes going into the first chicane and the Dutchman duly pounced.

His progress to maximum points thereafter was untroubled and, as he crossed the line, established a new standalone record for 10 consecutive Grands Prix victories.

It was a brief wait for confirmation of his third

Verstappen was truly king of the hill in 2023, his track dominance was a magnificent display – crushing his fellow drivers

Championship and it came in Qatar in October. Verstappen cruised to the win in the main race in the Gulf and although he was only third fastest over the 19 laps of the sprint race 24 hours earlier, Pérez's crash saw the Mexican fail to pick up any points to inadvertently seal the title for his team-mate. His third Championship on the bounce saw Verstappen become only the fifth driver ever after Fangio, Schumacher, Vettel and Hamilton to register the fabled hat-trick.

The statistics behind Verstappen's season were simply sensational. The 26-year-old's astonishing 19 triumphs in 22 races eclipsed his own previous milestone of 15 set in 2022 (an unprecedented 86.4% win ratio) while his 15 poles for the year surpassed the old record of 14 held by Nigel Mansell since 1992. Overall he scored 575 of the 620 points on offer, finishing a remarkable 290 points ahead of runner-up Pérez. Little wonder then that Verstappen himself rated his 2023 success as the greatest of his three world crowns. "This one is the best one," he admitted. "I think the first one was the most emotional one, because that's when your dreams are fulfilled. But this one has definitely been my best year."

It was a similar story of unchallenged supremacy for Red Bull as they defended the Constructors' Championship crown, securing a sixth title overall. With 21 wins in 22 races – Sainz in his Ferrari in Singapore the only driver to break the Red Bull stranglehold – the team set a new F1 record for a season. It was a staggering win ratio of over 95% and bettered the previous record of 19 chequered flags, albeit in 21 rather than 22 races, set by old rivals Mercedes in 2019.

From a neutral perspective, the 2024 season needed a renewed sense of jeopardy given Verstappen's undisputed dominance 12 months earlier and although the Dutchman ultimately emerged as the champion for a fourth time, the challenge the sport desperately craved did materialise in the form of McLaren's Lando Norris.

A Verstappen–Norris duel for the honours however seemed an unlikely scenario in the early stages of the season. The Dutch driver began the defence of his crown with four wins in the opening five weekends – a sequence only interrupted in Australia when the brakes

Verstappen amongst his orange army of fans at the Dutch Grand Prix, 2024

Lando Norris gets soaked in champagne after winning the 2024 Dutch Grand Prix, beating Max Verstappen in second place and Charles Leclerc third

on his Red Bull caught fire and forced him to retire – while Norris struggled with a solitary podium finish in his first four outings. The campaign though began to pivot in May at the Miami Grand Prix as Norris capitalised on the deployment of a safety car at the halfway point to pit, reappearing in first place before visibly outpacing the pursuing Verstappen. Victory in Florida was the first Grand Prix win in the 110th race of his career.

Buoyed by his maiden F1 success, Norris grew in stature while Verstappen and his Red Bull gradually began to look less, if only marginally, imperious. The four-time champion never relinquished his Championship lead but Norris continued to chip away and between the Austrian Grand Prix in June and Mexico in October, Verstappen endured a 10-race winless sequence while the Briton took the chequered flag in the Netherlands and Singapore. After the Mexican Grand Prix, the Dutch driver's advantage had been reduced to 47 points and with four races remaining the title race was still alive and kicking.

The question marks over Verstappen's coronation as a four-time world champion were finally dispelled after the Las Vegas Grand Prix at the end of November. George Russell claimed the win in Nevada from pole, Hamilton securing a one-two for Mercedes, while Verstappen's fifth and Norris's sixth confirmed the Red Bull star had become only the sixth man in history to celebrate a famous fourth Formula One driver's crown.

At face value, Verstappen's triumph may have suggested business as usual in 2024 but the Constructors' Championship standings painted an intriguingly different picture ahead of 2025. The dethroning of Red Bull, relegated to third, was the headline news as McLaren claimed the title for the ninth time and their first since in 26 frustrating years. Success for Andrea Stella's team was even more significant given finally it broke the Mercedes–Red Bull duopoly on the title, which dated back to 2009 when Brawn had been all conquering. Ferrari finished the year as runners-up and with Hamilton signing for the Prancing Horse, coupled with McLaren's resurgence and Red Bull's relative struggles, 2025 promised to be one of the most fiercely contested seasons in recent memory.

Norris at the British Grand Prix, 2024. He gave Max a run for his money in the driver's Championship and helped McLaren win the Constructors' title

Max Verstappen overtakes Lewis Hamilton and clinches a win at the Malaysian Grand Prix, 2017

«

Nico Rosberg beat Lewis Hamilton to the Championship for Mercedes in 2016

»

Lewis Hamilton in true blistering form, Japan 2018

Seb Vettel wins for Ferrari at the Canadian Grand Prix, 2018

Sparks fly for Alex Albon at the 2019 Japanese Grand Prix

Max Verstappen with another victory under his belt, 2019

Verstappen wins in Austria 2021, in front of his adoring crowd

Lewis Hamilton celebrates winning in Russia 2021, which turned out to be his mind-blowing 100th Grand Prix victory

Using his supreme skills going into a corner, Lando Norris in his McLaren, 2024

TOP TO MIDDLE: Showing quality, Mercedes driver George Russell

From Monaco, the naturally gifted Ferrari driver Charles Leclerc

Emerging Australian talent, McLaren's Oscar Piastri

Verstappen majestically sweeps into action at the British Grand Prix, 2024

Legendary
DRIVERS

LEWIS HAMILTON

F1'S BILLION DOLLAR MAN

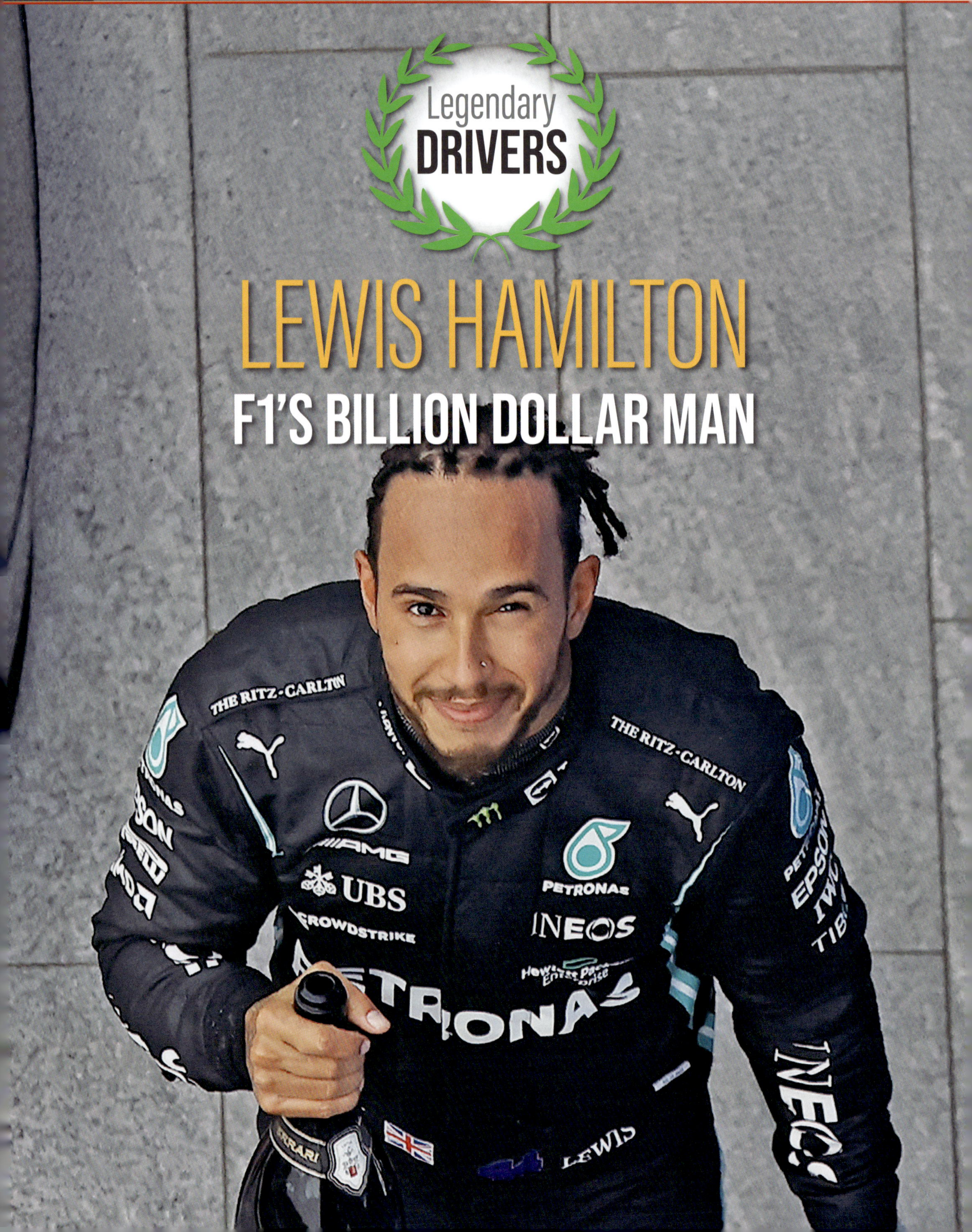

Unrivalled in his field, the boy who would receive a knighthood always knew he was destined for the summit of motorsport

It all started with a bold introduction. It was 3 December 1995 and Ron Dennis, multi-millionaire CEO and founder of the McLaren Group, was attending the Autosport Awards at the Grosvenor House Hotel on Park Lane in London when he felt someone tap him on the side. He turned round to be greeted by a beaming ten-year-old boy dressed in a smart suit.

"Hi. I'm Lewis Hamilton. I won the British Championship and one day I want to be racing your cars."

The boy who'd introduced himself as Lewis was clutching a booklet, which he now offered to Dennis with a polite request for his autograph and phone number, as he had done with a host of other stars that his father, Anthony, had been helping him to identify. It was a moment that Hamilton would later recall as an adult with a smile.

"My dad made this leather-bound booklet and he printed out all these pages in it, and then there was a space for the autograph, phone number and address of each individual. I remember when I was going around and saying, 'Please can you put your phone number down?' And I got phone numbers from, like, everyone at the place basically.

"So, my dad goes, 'That's Ron Dennis over there, he's the boss of McLaren that makes those cars that you love.' I knew immediately at that point, that's who Ayrton drives for and that's who I want to drive for. So, literally, before my dad had finished explaining to me about Ron Dennis, I went over to him straight away. I don't know what possessed me... where I had the confidence at the time to be able to say those things, but I guess naturally kids have lots of confidence or don't have any fear."

Impressed by his audacious yet charming new acquaintance, Dennis took the booklet and scribbled a note inside. "Phone me in nine years, we'll sort something out then." The offer was a genuine one, but Dennis could never have dreamed that it would one day bear fruit in the form of a world championship-winning driver. First, young Hamilton would have to prove himself on the track, a journey he embarked on in 1993, racing in karting competitions.

NEW KID ON THE GRID

Born in Stevenage in Hertfordshire, England, on 7 January 1985 to Anthony Hamilton and Carmen Larbalestier, Hamilton's first taste of racing came when his father bought him a radio-controlled car. Taking to racing instantly, Hamilton proved a skilled competitor, and the following year he bested adult rivals to finish second in the national BRCA Championship. Surprised by how rapidly his son had adapted to the rigours of racing, Anthony wondered if Lewis would prove equally adept at racing a full-size motor car.

At six years old, Hamilton received a go-kart for Christmas along with a promise that would transform his life. His father vowed that, provided he continued to apply himself at school, he would support his racing career in any way he could. At times this saw Anthony juggling up to four jobs in order to pay the bills and fund his son's fledgling career.

By 1993, eight-year-old Hamilton was ready to test himself against his fellow go-karters. Any concerns about how he'd fare on the tarmac quickly dissipated as Hamilton racked up numerous wins, victories that in turn led to cadet championship titles. Yet these remarkable achievements were eclipsed in 1995 when Hamilton became the youngest winner of the British Karting Championship. Further glory arrived in 1996 as Hamilton raced to victory in the Champions of the Future series (a crown he would successfully defend in 1997). He also managed to fend off rivals to become Five Nations and Sky TV KartMasters champion. Hamilton had overcome racist taunts from fellow racers and ferocious competition on the tracks to establish himself as a major talent in the world of motorsport, and his upward trajectory had not gone unnoticed.

Celebrations for another Hamilton podium, Russia 2021

TORQUE OF THE TOWN

Such was Hamilton's meteoric rise that some punters in the know were happy to place bets on the promising young driver (12 at the time) winning a world championship before turning 25. Yet more importantly than the whisperings and knowing nods occurring in betting shops was the fact that a key player in the industry had also been observing Hamilton's efforts from afar: Ron Dennis.

In 1998, just three years after first encountering him on that fateful night in London, Dennis decided to beat Hamilton to the punch and call him, and he wasn't just ringing to congratulate him on his glittering racing career. He was calling with a life-changing offer: a place in the McLaren development programme. The Hamilton family gladly accepted.

The youngest driver to receive a contract that would lead to competing in F1, Hamilton now had the backing of one of the biggest names in racing. He instantly repaid Dennis's faith (not to mention the sacrifices of his father) by progressing up the ranks and carving out further victories at Intercontinental A, Formula A and Formula Super A level. While racing in the latter two, Hamilton would meet Nico Rosberg for the first time, a German-Finnish teammate who would one day fight him for the ultimate prize.

World and European titles further cemented his place as a rising star (a status the British Racing Driver's Club officially recognised in 2000), but arguably the most exciting chapter in Hamilton's journey to date came in 2001, when he competed in a one-off go-kart race that featured a special guest: four-time world champion Michael Schumacher. Finishing a mere four places behind the German, Hamilton earned the highest of praise from the only other man to win seven world titles: "He's a quality driver, very strong and only 16. If he keeps this up I'm sure he will reach F1." By 2007, at just 22, Hamilton would fulfil Schumacher's prophecy after spells in Formula 3 and GP2.

KING OF THE WORLD

As the 2007 season loomed, McLaren found themselves with a vacancy. Colombian Juan Pablo Montoya's decision to head to America to compete in NASCAR, combined with Finnish racer Kimi Räikkönen's transfer to Ferrari (with whom he'd win the 2007 world championship) left McLaren in need of a partner for two-time champion Fernando Alonso. After some deliberation, McLaren informed Hamilton that he would be the team's new driver.

"We reviewed the whole grid, and when we looked at the drivers other than the top three, there was no one that really shone," said Dennis. "Lewis has been in the family for a long time and he deserves the opportunity we're giving him." It would prove to be a chance that the young talent would eagerly grab with both gloved hands.

As unfazed as the boy who had stormed the world of karting over a decade before, Hamilton wasted no time in making an impression as he surged to a third-place

Ron Dennis (right) was instrumental in giving Hamilton a seat in Formula 1

finish to snatch a spot on the podium in his debut race at the Australian Grand Prix. Incredibly, he'd repeat the feat nine times in a row in a record-breaking rookie season, a string of astonishing finishes that included victories in Canada and the US (the first time a British driver had won a grand prix in the States since 1983). The youngest driver to ever sit at the summit of a world championship, Hamilton was flourishing at the highest level of motorsport, and while his bid for immortality was ultimately derailed by a puncture in Turkey and the snare of a gravel trap in China, finishing one point behind eventual champion Räikkönen was an unbelievable achievement and a portent of things to come.

Hamilton is widely regarded as one of the most talented drivers ever to grace a track, but behind his supreme ability lies an endless dedication to improving his craft and a level of consistency that few others can hope to match. Yet bizarrely his maiden world championship title in 2008 would be built on flashes of brilliance and moments of genius that punctuated an otherwise error-strewn season.

Everything started promisingly, with victory in Australia. But then a penalty in Malaysia was compounded by a crash in Canada, Hamilton careering into Räikkönen as the Finn waited at a red light. Additional misjudgements (some committed by the McLaren team) dogged Hamilton in Belgium and also Japan, as Stevenage's most famous son battled to keep his campaign from skidding off track.

The highlight of 2008 – and, according to many experts and pundits, his career to date – came on the rain-drenched track at Silverstone on an unforgettable July afternoon. Despite starting from fourth on the grid and facing horrendous conditions, Hamilton displayed his now famous mastery of the elements to annihilate the competition and take the chequered flag a full minute before Nick Heidfeld of BMW Sauber crossed the finish line. It would prove to be a crucial victory.

By the time the world of Formula 1 was gearing up for the season's climax in Brazil on 2 November, Hamilton had managed to notch up additional wins in both Germany and China to put himself top of the championship table by seven points. However, home favourite Felipe Massa lurked close behind, poised to drive Ferrari to victory and secure his place in the annals of F1 history.

In sixth place on the grid, Hamilton's task was clear: gain a single place and hold it. That is all it would take to make him the youngest – not to mention the first Black – F1 world champion, yet by the last lap he remained in sixth. Massa looked destined to take the crown. Nearing the final bend, Hamilton steeled himself for a manoeuvre that could secure glory or send him spinning into the nearest barrier. With Sebastian Vettel screaming along beside him, Hamilton lunged, overtaking Toyota's Timo Glock to pinch fifth place and the title in dramatic style. The boy who'd idolised Ayrton Senna as a child and confidently introduced himself to the head of McLaren had fulfilled his greatest dreams. The only Black man ever to compete in F1 had overcome seemingly insurmountable odds to stand unrivalled at the summit of a championship that had not been won by a fellow Brit since Damon Hill in 1996. But perhaps most importantly of all, he'd repaid his father's endless sacrifices, all those hours working numerous jobs, the countless drives to competitions and his unwavering support in the finest way possible.

Hamilton (left) rounds the bend to overtake Kovalainen at a rain-soaked British Grand Prix, 2008

A TEST OF VETTEL

Given his astounding exploits in the previous two seasons, it was tempting to assume as the 2009 F1 season loomed that Hamilton would successfully defend his history-making title. In reality he never came close to repeating his 2008 triumph as his season began in the worst possible fashion.

After fighting his way up to fourth place from 18th in the opening Australian Grand Prix, Hamilton (with the knowledge of his team) permitted Toyota's Italian driver Jarno Trulli to speed past when a safety car was present on the track, an overtaking that they knew would result in a penalty for Trulli. Denying any wrongdoing to race officials, McLaren were quickly undermined by the emergence of radio communications that exposed the duplicity. For his part in the debacle Hamilton was disqualified in what he later called "the hardest week of my life" – so hard that he briefly wondered if stepping down from F1 was the gracious thing to do. Thankfully for the sport he eventually disregarded the notion, but the fact that he even considered it is testament to the toll the whole episode took on the young star.

To compound his misery, a string of poor results on the track turned an unwelcome spotlight on the condition of the MP4-24, a car that was lambasted as being "possibly the worst car McLaren has ever designed". Even a series of much-needed improvements couldn't reverse the team's fortunes, and despite wins in Hungary and Singapore, Hamilton finished a distant fifth behind eventual champion Jenson Button. To Hamilton and McLaren's frustration, finishing some way off the top would become a regular occurrence in the following years as a new, more robust threat emerged: Sebastian Vettel.

After promising spells at BMW Sauber and Toro Rosso, Vettel had moved to Red Bull in 2009, a move that would reap remarkable rewards for both parties. The German's first season almost ended in instant triumph as he finished 11 points behind Button in the final standings, a result that evidently spurred the 22 year old to chase greater heights. For the next four seasons the Heppenheim hotshot would utterly dominate the world of F1, eclipsing Hamilton in 2010 to become the youngest-ever world champion and then maintaining an iron grip on the trophy in 2011, 2012 and 2013. It seemed as though Red Bull would rule the tarmac for years to come.

Throughout Vettel's reign at the peak of motorsport, Hamilton finished no higher than fourth, dipping back down to fifth in a 2011 season peppered with fiery clashes that saw him smash into Red Bull's Mark Webber and Sauber's Kamui Kobayashi among others. Arguably the nadir of a poor season came on 29 May in Monaco, when he responded to a brace of penalties by accusing officials of hounding him due to the colour of his skin, comments he later retracted. Hamilton would finish the season behind a teammate for the first time as Button finished second behind Vettel, 43 points ahead of Hamilton.

Hamilton and old foe Fernando Alonso collide and crash out at the first corner of the Belgian Grand Prix, 2012

Lewis Hamilton and teammate Nico Rosberg fight it out on track at the 'Duel in the Desert' – the 2014 Bahrain Grand Prix

KEEP YOUR ENEMIES CLOSE

After a year spent struggling, 2012 witnessed some improvement as Hamilton raced to wins in Canada, Hungary, Italy and the US, but his fourth-placed finish in the final standings was overshadowed by the shocking revelation that he would be terminating his association with McLaren and moving to Mercedes in time for the 2013 season. By putting his name to a three-year deal with his new employers, Hamilton was securing a reunion with his childhood teammate Nico Rosberg, setting the stage for a gripping rivalry.

The move didn't immediately pay dividends for Mercedes, as Hamilton could only manage a solitary victory in Hungary (as well as several podium finishes), but it wouldn't be long before their newest recruit began to prove why they had spent big money to lure him away from McLaren, and both parties would be helped by a mandate issued by the F1 authorities that stipulated the use of turbo-hybrid engines.

Mastering the intricacies of this type of engine better than any rival outfit, Mercedes constructed a car that perfectly suited Hamilton's skillset, setting him up to completely dominate the 2014 season with 11 wins and a second world title. He would enjoy further success in the following season, racking up ten wins and a record-equalling 17 podium finishes to sweep to his third Drivers' Championship. However, 2016 would go the way of Rosberg, who snatched the title in the final race of the season in Abu Dhabi before stunning the world by announcing his retirement at just 31. "I have climbed my mountain, I am on the peak, so this feels right," Rosberg explained.

GLOBAL DOMINATION

In the wake of Rosberg's sudden departure, Hamilton publicly admitted that he "didn't care" who replaced him. Ultimately, he was right not to, as the arrival of Valtteri Bottas had no impact on the final outcome of the 2017 season. Nobody was stopping Hamilton, who seized another world title courtesy of nine wins, including a stellar drive in Spain in which he recovered from kissing wheels with Vettel and sliding off the track to overtake the German and hold on for victory.

Hamilton was equally untouchable in 2018 as he notched a record 408 points in a single season to retain his crown, finishing 88 clear of Vettel thanks to 11 wins and a remarkable 17 podium finishes once again. Eager to retain his services, Mercedes rewarded Hamilton with a £40-million two-year extension. The investment was promptly repaid in 2019 with a third successive title,

clinched with a new record points haul of 413.

Of his 11 victories that season, Monaco was his finest, where he had to hold off a promising young rival by the name of Max Verstappen. An exhausted Hamilton said afterwards, "I think it was the hardest race I've had… It was the biggest challenge I think I've had and I'm really grateful I was able to pull it off."

It seemed like it would take something of biblical proportions to stop Hamilton from continuing to dominate F1. In early 2020 it arrived in the form of the COVID-19 pandemic, which saw the new season postponed from March to July and eventually condensed to 17 races. No matter: Hamilton would storm to 11 wins again to secure a record-equalling seventh world title to put him level with Michael Schumacher. His most impressive victory came in Turkey as he overcame torrential rain to finish 30 seconds ahead of Bottas, a cleverly timed switch from wet tyres to intermediates propelling him to glory.

For four straight years nobody had managed to get near Hamilton. Sure, there had been drivers who occasionally threatened to pull level or force him to find a higher gear, but eventually all had faded away into Hamilton's slipstream, condemned to acquaint themselves with the rear of his car. There was no reason to expect that 2021 would be any different.

MAD MAX AND AN UPSET IN THE UAE

Beginning in Bahrain on 28 March, the 2021 season opened in familiar style as Hamilton screeched to his 96th career victory, becoming the first driver in F1 history to thereby win at least one race in each season they had competed in. Verstappen would immediately reply with victory in the Italian Grand Prix in week two, but a brace of Hamilton victories in Portugal and Spain quickly restored order. However, anyone who discounted Verstappen's chances at this point would be proved spectacularly wrong as the young Dutchman hit back again to notch victory in Monaco. F1 had a battle on its hands once more.

Over the course of the season, Hamilton and Verstappen regularly exchanged places at the top of the table, and by the final weekend of the season in December they had banked eight and nine wins respectively. The last race, set to be hosted in Abu Dhabi, would decide the winner.

Prior to the race, Verstappen had managed to secure pole position on the grid, with Hamilton just behind him in second. When the green light flashed a ferocious contest ensued, in which several cars either crashed or were forced to retire due to mechanical issues. Hamilton worked hard to hunt Verstappen down and then carve out a hefty time advantage as he muscled his way into first.

With just five of the 58 laps to go, a crash on turn 14 spelled the arrival of a safety car. Mercedes and Hamilton decided to keep the reigning world champion out on the track in order to maintain his position, but Verstappen took the opportunity to switch to softer tyres. Even so, five cars sat between him and Hamilton, who only had to try and hold on for the last few circuits to be able to clinch a record-breaking eighth championship.

Initially, race director Michael Masi stated that the five cars between the rivals could not pass the safety car and unlap themselves, maintaining the obstacle preventing Verstappen from pulling level with Hamilton. Then Masi changed his mind and announced that the five interlopers could in fact unlap themselves. This decision effectively cleared the route for Verstappen

Verstappen overtakes Hamilton to take the race win and become World Champion – to the dismay and horror of the Mercedes team, Abu Dhabi Grand Prix, 2021

to speed towards Hamilton, who he duly managed to overtake and then hold off to secure his maiden world title amid a hail of complaints from Mercedes. "Michael this isn't right. Michael!" bellowed Toto Wolff to no avail. Victory had been snatched away, a result that would subsequently be confirmed when Mercedes' appeal against the decision was dismissed. In his typically humble way, Hamilton congratulated Verstappen in post-race interviews, while also praising the efforts of everyone on team Mercedes.

ARISE, SIR LEWIS

Losing out on an eighth world championship understandably hit Hamilton hard, and rumours circulated that the perceived injustice of Verstappen's triumph may convince Hamilton to retire, although Mercedes were quick to dismiss the idea that Hamilton wouldn't bid for the title in 2022. Yet the opening race in Bahrain on 20 March loomed ever closer without a definitive answer. Could arguably the greatest F1 driver in history really be poised to step away from the sport that had defined his life and propelled him to greatness?

Hamilton's appearance at the launch of Mercedes' car for the 2022 season finally put an end to the rumours. While his continued presence on the track had now been assured, what had always remained beyond doubt was Hamilton's place in the history books. A fashion icon and dedicated activist off the track, he was recognised for his achievements in the 2021 New Year's Honours list with a knighthood, a title bestowed upon him by Prince Charles at Windsor Castle just three days after his defeat in Abu Dhabi.

With Hamilton returning to the cockpit in 2022, the rivalry with Verstappen could shape Formula 1 for years to come. Every champion needs a worthy adversary, and Verstappen is shaping up to fulfil that role with aplomb. Even so, if Hamilton had ultimately chosen to end his career in racing, he would have done so safe in the knowledge that he had fulfilled his wildest dreams seven times over and cemented his place alongside the legends he used to watch as a child. Yet perhaps his greatest achievement was standing by his values and sticking to a promise he made to himself. "I don't aspire to be like other drivers – I aspire to be unique in my own way," he once said. Whatever the future holds, Sir Lewis Hamilton will continue to do things his way, and there is no better path to tread than your own.

In the immediate aftermath of what would have been a career-defining controversy in Abu Dhabi for a mere mortal driver, Hamilton largely kept his own counsel. He would later publicly claim he "was robbed" but with three brief months before the start of the 2022 season, he and Mercedes retreated over the winter to lick their collective wounds and plan their eagerly anticipated response to Hamilton's contentious loss of the Championship.

His off-season was punctuated by a visit to Windsor Castle in December where the sport's most prolific driver ever was knighted by the Prince of Wales. In receiving the award, Hamilton became the fourth F1 star to become a Sir after Jack Brabham, Jackie Stewart and Stirling Moss but unlike the illustrious trio who had proceeded, he was the first to receive the coveted royal recognition while still racing.

Fans who dreamed of another epic year of gladiatorial cut and thrust between the Brit and Verstappen in 2022, however, were to be sorely disappointed. The FIA's technical rule changes for the new season were described as the most significant

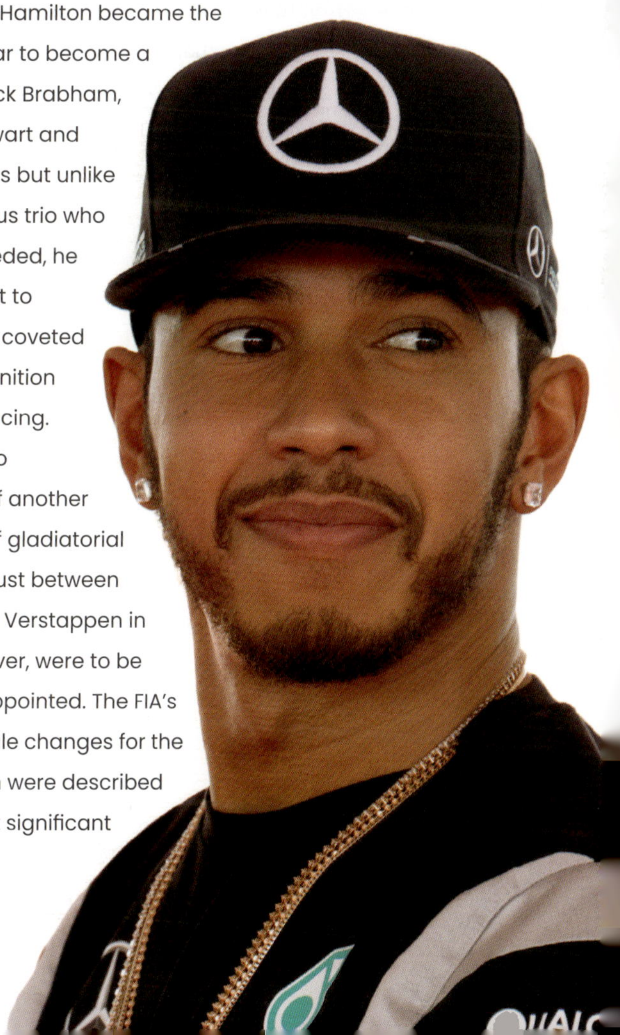

Where others may have faltered, Lewis kept a cool head after the anxious 2021 season finale

in the sport in two decades by Red Bull engineering supremo Adrian Newey, but Mercedes struggled to come to terms with the simplifications required to their cars' power units, as well as an overhaul of the aerodynamics around the chassis. The FIA's decision to remove Michael Masi as race director after his infamous intervention at the Yas Marina Circuit was one change ahead of 2022 which Mercedes, if only in private, did warmly welcome.

The year nonetheless was one to forget. Hamilton was joined at Mercedes by compatriot George Russell, signed from Williams, but the change in personnel failed to ignite the team as both cars startlingly lacked pace. Hamilton kicked off with a podium finish in Bahrain but as the 22 races came and went, it was all too apparent that the seven-time champion was not a serious challenger. His sixth place in the final standings, trailing 35 points behind his new team-mate, was the worst finish of his career and it was the first time in his 16 seasons in F1 that he failed to register a victory. To compound the dark mood, Mercedes were deposed as champion constructor by Red Bull, ending their historic eight-year reign as the undisputed kings of the paddock.

There was little in 2023 to dispel the sense of deep despondency in the Mercedes camp. Both driver and team made modest improvements, Hamilton was third overall while Mercedes leapfrogged Ferrari to finish as runners-up in Constructors' Championship, but it was ultimately a forlorn season in which Verstappen and Red Bull were repeatedly a mirage on the distant horizon.

It may have been a similar story in 2024, but the month after celebrating his 39th birthday, Hamilton rocked Formula One with the announcement he would drive for Ferrari the following season. The pantheon of greats to grace The Prancing Horse in Grands Prix is unrivalled but not even the arrival of then two-time title winner Michael Schumacher from Benetton in 1996 could compare to the coup of securing the services of Britain's serial champion. "It was obviously the hardest decision that I think I've ever had to make," Hamilton said after confirming 2024 would be his 12th and final season with Mercedes. "We've had an absolutely incredible journey together. We've created history within the sport. But I think ultimately I'm writing my story and I felt like it was time to start a new chapter."

Reaction to the shock news was as incredulous as it was widespread. "Hamilton's move to Ferrari is one of the biggest – and most surprising – stories in F1 for years,"

TOP TO BOTTOM: Lewis and George Russell being interviewed by Martin Brundle at Silverstone, 2022

Hamilton in the 2024 Mercedes

Red is the colour. Hamilton in his shiny new Ferrari, Japan 2025

wrote the BBC's Formula One correspondent Andrew Benson. "Hamilton has always insisted he wanted to spend the rest of his career and beyond with Mercedes – likening his situation to that of the late Stirling Moss, who was a Mercedes ambassador for his whole life. But things have changed and Hamilton has decided he cannot turn down the lure of Ferrari, whose history, legend and mystique is always a strong pull for any F1 driver.

"He remains the biggest star in F1, as well as its most successful ever driver. Hamilton was badly hurt by the events of the 2021 Abu Dhabi Grand Prix. He believes he was robbed of an eighth world title by race director Masi's failure to follow the rules correctly with the operation of a safety car late in that race. Since then, he has been driven by a desire to avenge that injustice – even if he has not quite put it that way in public."

For his legion of fans, the 2024 season for Hamilton became an exercise in marking time as he continued to struggle in his underpowered Mercedes. Seventh in the driver's standings was far from the fairy-tale farewell to the German team he would have wished for but there was the consolation of an emotional victory at the British Grand Prix in July, the first time he had taken the chequered flag since his win in Saudi Arabia in 2021. Sixteen years after his maiden victory on home soil, the result extended his record of career triumphs at Silverstone to nine and four clear of Alain Prost and Jim Clark.

Pioneer. Icon. Activist.

Although he will forever be known first and foremost for his achievements on the race track, Lewis Hamilton has an equally important role away from the world of F1 as an activist in the struggle against racism and inequality. As the only Black man to ever race at the highest level of motorsport, Hamilton unfortunately has first-hand experience of racism, something that he now works hard to combat by supporting movements such as Black Lives Matter and making his feelings known when cases of injustice surface, such as the killing of Breonna Taylor in March 2020.

As someone who also knew the harsh constraints of living in a family that struggled financially, in the summer of 2021 Hamilton founded Mission 44 (44 being the number he races under), to help children from underrepresented groups take their first steps in the world of motor racing, engineering, science, technology and maths. Injecting £20 million of his own money into the charity, Hamilton feels as though he has finally found his calling.

"Now I feel like I have a mission in life, and it's not about just winning championships and races – that's all cool – but actually being able to make an impact to help youngsters coming through."

Flanked by Verstappen and Vettel, Hamilton takes the knee in support of the fight against racism

Legendary DRIVERS

MAX VERSTAPPEN

SUPERMAX

The young gun who pushes to the limit and beyond in his quest for success

Most 17-year-olds struggle with driving lessons and the theory test. Max Verstappen was different. When the 2015 season kicked off in Australia, Verstappen qualified his Toro Rosso in 12th place at the tender age of 17 years and 166 days, beating the record for the youngest driver to start a Grand Prix by nearly two years. Two weeks later he qualified sixth and finished seventh to become the youngest points scorer. Just over a year later, Verstappen won his debut Grand Prix with Red Bull to become the youngest race winner.

The baby-faced assassin soon developed a reputation as a no-holds-barred racer. He demonstrated his bravery by storming around the outside of Nico Rosberg at a very wet 2016 Brazilian Grand Prix and made up for a poor start at the 2019 Austrian Grand Prix by picking off Charles Leclerc's Ferrari with two laps to go, tricking him with a dummy before pouncing on the inside. But Verstappen's aggression often came at a price. Felipe Massa branded Verstappen 'dangerous' after clipping the back of Romain Grosjean in Monaco in 2015, Kimi Räikkönen offered similar criticism in Belgium a year later and Esteban Ocon had an unseemly scuffle with Verstappen at the end of the 2018 Brazilian GP.

But by 2021, Verstappen had earned two third-place finishes in the Drivers' Championship and the F1 world was waiting for him to challenge Lewis Hamilton for the title. And he finally did. He took pole position in Bahrain, the first race of the season. Although Lewis Hamilton slipped by early on, Verstappen didn't give up. On lap 53, just four from the end, he overtook Hamilton but went off track while doing so. Race control ordered him to let Hamilton back past and Verstappen trailed him home in second place.

That Bahrain overtake was the first of many controversial events in a season that saw the fiercest rivalry develop since Senna and Prost. Verstappen and Hamilton traded places at the top of the standings and traded paint on the track. Verstappen's clumsy attempt to take the lead on the first lap of the British Grand Prix led to a collision with Hamilton. Although the Brit came out of it unscathed and went on to win the race, Verstappen slid sideways into a gravel trap and collided with a tyre wall at 290 km/h (180 mph). His race weekend ended with him

Max Verstappen was the sixth driver to take a seat at Red Bull after coming through their driver academy and the third to win a Grand Prix

Verstappen had his first race win at the Spanish Grand Prix in 2016

MIDDLE TO BOTTOM: A win for Max at the 2017 Malaysian Grand Prix, with Hamilton second and teammate Daniel Ricciardo third

Verstappen still makes the odd error now and then

being checked out at a local hospital. In Italy, Hamilton came out of the pits side by side with Verstappen. Neither man backed down as they raced through turns one and two. Verstappen was forced onto a kerb, clipped Hamilton's rear tyre and was launched into the air, landing on top of Hamilton's cockpit. Damage forced both drivers to retire and the post-race investigation deemed Verstappen to be most at fault. Were it not for the newly introduced halo device, the crash could have cost Hamilton far more than a few championship points.

But Verstappen also showed his sheer speed and skill when he had the luxury of driving in clean air without Hamilton around. He took his first grand slam at the Austrian Grand Prix, taking pole position, leading the race from start to finish and setting the fastest lap. And although it seemed he had been around for ages, Verstappen set a new record as the youngest driver to achieve a grand slam.

Ultimately, the Drivers' Championship came down to the final lap of the final race. And, surprise, surprise, there was controversy involved. When a crash brought out the safety car with five laps to go, second-placed Verstappen pitted for fresh tyres. Hamilton did not pit, as it would have sacrificed the lead. But then, race director Michael Masi made two questionable calls. He allowed the five cars between Hamilton and Verstappen to unlap themselves – but only those five. And he insisted there was time for a one-lap run-off. Verstappen used his fresh tyres to

Italian Grand Prix drama! Max Verstappen and Lewis Hamilton's battle for the 2021 World Championship was one of the most thrilling in recent years

overtake and take the title by eight points. Cue wild celebrations in the Low Countries and howls of outrage from Lewis Hamilton fans.

Though the circumstances of that race and the season as a whole were marred by controversy, Verstappen had finally become world champion for the first time. It was a destiny many had expected him to fulfil since watching his teenage debut.

Even if some claim there is an asterisk in the history books next to his first Drivers' Championship title, nobody can deny he was a worthy winner of his second, because Verstappen retained the Drivers' Championship in 2022 by a comfortable margin. Although he suffered two retirements in the first three races as Red Bull struggled with their fuel system, Verstappen benefited from the performance of Hamilton's Mercedes falling off a cliff. Verstappen's main rival in 2022 would be Ferrari's Charles Leclerc, but he was usually a distant challenger.

Verstappen sliced Leclerc's early-season championship lead at the fourth round, the Emilia Romagna Grand Prix, when he scored his second grand slam of flag-to-flag race win, fastest lap and pole position. That was the first of five wins from the next six races; his only failure came when teammate Sergio Pérez kept him off the top step in Monaco. Then, Verstappen won five in a row between rounds 12 and 16.

The title came his way at the end of the Japanese Grand Prix, when there were still six races to run. And as if to remind F1 watchers that nothing is simple when Verstappen is involved, he was crowned in unusual circumstances. The race started in heavy rain and was red flagged after two laps, with Verstappen retaining the lead from pole. After a long break, the race resumed behind the safety car before it eventually pulled off for a brief period of live racing, but the chequered flag was waved after 28 laps due to the race passing its three-hour time limit. Verstappen returned to the pits thinking he would be awarded half points for winning the shortened race, but the race officials decided that full points were on offer. They then gave Leclerc a five-second penalty for cutting a chicane, dropping him to third place. Verstappen now had an insurmountable 113-point lead in the Drivers' Championship. Once again,

Max at the British Grand Prix, 2022

he had won the season-long race for points due to a race official's decision.

But he would have won the title had the officials not intervened, because the stats for Verstappen's second championship-winning season were stunning. He won 15 of 22 races with seven pole positions and five fastest laps. It was the most race wins in a single season, breaking the mark of 13 set by Michael Schumacher in 2004 and Sebastian Vettel in 2013. When he didn't win, he finished on the podium in two of the other seven races. That helped him to a total of 454 points, breaking the previous record of 413 set by Lewis Hamilton in 2019. And unlike 2021, when Mercedes were the winning constructor, Verstappen and Pérez combined to give Red Bull a blistering 205-point margin over Ferrari in the Constructors' Championship.

Recent Formula 1 history has tended to run in eras in which one driver dominates. Michael Schumacher was the man in the early 2000s. Then came Sebastian Vettel in the early 2010s, then Lewis Hamilton to end the decade. Are we now seeing another changing of the guard? Few would be surprised if, a decade from now, Verstappen has matched – or even surpassed – his illustrious compatriots.

Despite the imperious style of his second Championship triumph, many F1 insiders suspected Verstappen was only just getting started and as he sat on pole for the start of the season-opening Bahrain Grand Prix in 2023, the 25-year-old must have believed a hat-trick of consecutive crowns – only ever achieved four times previously in the sport's history – was firmly within his grasp. Whether even Verstappen could have envisaged the stunning and unprecedented way he would complete the feat is moot.

The Dutch driver lead almost exclusively from start to finish in Bahrain to take the chequered flag, his maiden win in Sakhir, and maximum points. The rest of the season rapidly became a procession that showcased both his outrageous talent and his Red Bull's indisputable technical superiority, while the sport's overworked historians were forced to rapidly and repeatedly update the record books.

His 10 successive Grand Prix victories, beginning in Miami in May and climaxing with a win in Italy at Monza four months later, is a milestone that may never be eclipsed. The Dutchman's scarcely-believable tally of 19 chequered flags during 2023 is another record which it is difficult to imagine any driver improving in a single season while his accumulated haul of 575 points and the final winning margin – he finished an astonishing 290 points clear of runner-up Pérez – are statistics which will surely have future generations checking suspiciously

Verstappen with title contnder Lando Norris in his wake, Dutch Grand Prix, 2024

2024, another World Championship for the Red Bull star

whether the record books had been updated in error.

"From pre-season testing it was clear Max was going to win the title, but few expected it to be wrapped up so early, and with such dominant statistics in terms of victories and laps led," said Phil Horton of the *New York Times*. "He has always had the raw speed, but now he has vast experience, allied with the assurance that he has long since achieved everything he wanted in Formula 1 – and more. Yet, as Red Bull boss Christian Horner outlined, he retains a voracious appetite not just to succeed but to dominate."

That seemingly insatiable hunger was again evident in 2024. Verstappen was perhaps unsurprisingly unable to replicate quite the unqualified dominance that he had enjoyed the previous year, chiefly due to the emergence of Lando Norris in his McLaren as a genuine threat, but the reigning champion was still head and shoulders above the rest of the field. Seven poles in the first seven races, yielding five wins, set a familiar tone for the campaign and he was never overtaken in the overall table from the start of proceedings. He became a four-time world champion at Las Vegas Grand Prix in October, finishing fifth to seal the title and join an exclusive club, boasting members Alain Prost and Sebastian Vettel, that only admits four-time Formula One world champions.

Whether Verstappen can one day rival Hamilton and Michael Schumacher's record of seven crowns is a matter of opinion. Formula One can be unpredictable but the Dutch star, in theory at least, could achieve the feat only months after marking his 30th birthday.

Motorsport in the Blood

He may be known as the Flying Dutchman, but Max Verstappen was actually born in Hasselt, a city in Belgium near the Dutch border. And his family pedigree ensured there was never a doubt that young Max would be a racer. His mother, Sophie Kumpen, competed successfully in karting. Her cousin, Anthony Kumpen, is a two-time NASCAR Whelen Euro Series champion, and her uncle, Paul Kumpen, is a former motocross and endurance rally driver.

But F1 fans of a certain age will most remember Max's father, Jos Verstappen, who competed in the most prestigious form of motorsport over eight seasons for seven different teams. Jos made his debut in 1994 when he stepped in for the injured JJ Lehto for Benetton. It was an eventful debut – Jos somersaulted his car after being forced onto the grass and grazed the helmet of Martin Brundle in an eerie premonition of the time his son's car would almost make contact with the helmet of Lewis Hamilton. Later that season, fuel leaked onto Verstappen's car during a pitstop and it was briefly engulfed in a fireball. Both times, Jos was unhurt.

Jos remained in F1 but changed teams every season for the next five years: to Simtek, Arrows, Tyrrell, Stewart and Honda. He returned to Arrows, before finishing his career with Minardi. He never troubled the F1 podium beyond two consecutive third-place finishes in his season with Benetton, but he is in the relatively exclusive 100-plus Grand Prix club.

Jos and his wife separated when Max was a child, but he coached Max and attended his son's races whenever his own racing schedule allowed. Max chooses to compete with a Dutch racing license because he spent so much time competing in kart races over the border in the Netherlands with his father by his side.

Verstappen's father Jos was a journeyman driver who competed in 106 Grands Prix for six different teams

EPILOGUE

The drama and unpredictability of the history of Formula One belies the fact that the sport's story has always been one of periods of mesmeric dominance. The legendary Juan Manuel Fangio established the pattern with his five titles in seven years in the 1950s and ever since the Argentinian's famous exploits put F1 on the sporting map, successive generations have witnessed a driver inexorably rise above their mere mortal rivals and write their name into the record books.

Iconic Frenchman Alain Prost was Fangio's all-conquering heir apparent with his four Championship triumphs, the first sealed in 1985, but even his remarkable feats were eclipsed, first by Michael Schumacher and then by compatriot Sebastian Vettel. Lewis Hamilton more recently picked up the baton with his record-equalling seven titles and now Formula One has a new, seemingly untouchable trailblazer in Max Verstappen with his quartet of consecutive crowns and counting.

The burning question is whether the Dutchman can again sweep the competition aside or will a different name, new or more familiar, be etched on the winner's trophy by the end of the 2025 season?

Liam Lawson in a Formula 3 race, 2019. In a bizarre twist of events instigated by team advisor Helmut Marko, Liam Lawson lost his seat in the Red Bull and returned to the sister team, Racing Bulls

Hope springs eternal for the chasing pack. The dethroning of Red Bull as the champion constructor by McLaren suggests the four-time champion will have a fight on his hands. Championship runner-up Lando Norris posted his maiden GP victory in 2024, the first of four over the course of a breakthrough season, and at the age of 25 is rapidly approaching the peak of his powers. Meanwhile waiting in the wings his McLaren teammate Australian Oscar Piastri also notched two wins, maybe a sign of greater things to come.

Red however could yet be the colour if Hamilton's dramatic switch to Ferrari reaps the rewards the Italian

team so desperately crave. It has been 17 frustrating years since The Prancing Horse last secured a championship, but they pushed McLaren agonisingly close in 2024 and look well placed to mount another concerted challenge. At the age of 35 years and 313 days, Hamilton became F1's oldest champion of the 21st century with his 2020 title win, and desperate to sit in glorious isolation as an eight-time world champion, one clear of Schumacher, motivation for the now 40-year-old will not be in short supply.

The fortunes of the younger generation of drivers will be fascinating to follow. In a u-turn, Racing Bulls driver New Zealander Liam Lawson had to make way for Yuki Tsunoda from Japan as Verstappen's latest Red Bull partner, both potential threats. Young Italian rookie 18-year-old Kimi Antonelli is a relative unknown in Grand Prix motor racing who has joined Mercedes as George Russell's teammate. Russell outperformed Hamilton at Mercedes in 2024, hinting at perhaps even greater things to come from the British driver.

Now in his eighth F1 campaign, his seventh for Ferrari, Charles Leclerc has always had the innate talent to challenge and will still harbour dreams of emulating compatriot Prost and taking the trophy back to France.

As ever in Formula One, the champion will ultimately be decided by the mercurial marriage of man and machine. Verstappen remains the driver to beat, but whether he and his Red Bull can combine for a fifth successive year and be dominant once again is far from a foregone conclusion as the sport celebrates its milestone 75th anniversary.

McLaren's Lando Norris proved he could be a race winner in 2024

INSET: Oscar Piastri, who makes up a mouthwatering duo for Mclaren in 2025

TOP TO BOTTOM: Yuki Tsunoda at the Spanish Grand Prix, 2024

Teenager Kimi Antonelli in a Formula 2 race in 2024

FORMULA ONE STATISTICS & RECORDS

The history-making, record-breaking Grand Prix drivers and constructors who have lit up the first 75 years of Formula One racing

DRIVERS' WORLD CHAMPIONSHIP WINNERS

Year	Drivers	Country	Team	Wins	Points
1950	Guiseppe Farina	Italy	Alfa Romeo	3	30
1951	Juan Manuel Fangio	Argentina	Alfa Romeo	3	31
1952	Alberto Ascari	Italy	Ferrari	6	36
1953	Alberto Ascari	Italy	Ferrari	5	34.5
1954	Juan Manuel Fangio	Argentina	Maserati/Mercedes	6	42
1955	Juan Manuel Fangio	Argentina	Mercedes	4	40
1956	Juan Manuel Fangio	Argentina	Ferrari	3	30
1957	Juan Manuel Fangio	Argentina	Maserati	4	40
1958	Mike Hawthorn	UK	Ferrari	1	42
1959	Jack Brabham	Australia	Cooper	2	31
1960	Jack Brabham	Australia	Cooper	5	43
1961	Phil Hill	USA	Ferrari	2	34
1962	Graham Hill	UK	BRM	2	42
1963	Jim Clark	UK	Lotus	7	54
1964	John Surtees	UK	Ferrari	2	40
1965	Jim Clark	UK	Lotus	6	54
1966	Jack Brabham	Australia	Brabham	4	42
1967	Denny Hulme	New Zealand	Brabham	2	51
1968	Graham Hill	UK	Lotus	3	48
1969	Jackie Stewart	UK	Matra	6	63
1970	Jochen Rindt	Austria	Lotus	5	45
1971	Jackie Stewart	UK	Tyrrell	6	62
1972	Emerson Fittipaldi	Brazil	Lotus	5	61
1973	Jackie Stewart	UK	Tyrrell	5	71
1974	Emerson Fittipaldi	Brazil	McLaren	3	55
1975	Niki Lauda	Austria	Ferrari	5	64.5
1976	James Hunt	UK	McLaren	6	69
1977	Niki Lauda	Austria	Ferrari	3	72
1978	Mario Andretti	USA	Lotus	6	64
1979	Jody Scheckter	South Africa	Ferrari	3	51
1980	Alan Jones	Australia	Williams	5	67

Year	Drivers	Country	Team	Wins	Points
1981	Nelson Piquet	Brazil	Brabham	3	50
1982	Keke Rosberg	Finland	Williams	1	44
1983	Nelson Piquet	Brazil	Brabham	3	59
1984	Niki Lauda	Austria	McLaren	5	72
1985	Alain Prost	France	McLaren	5	73
1986	Alain Prost	France	McLaren	4	72
1987	Nelson Piquet	Brazil	Williams	3	73
1988	Ayrton Senna	Brazil	McLaren	8	90
1989	Alain Prost	France	McLaren	4	76
1990	Ayrton Senna	Brazil	McLaren	6	78
1991	Ayrton Senna	Brazil	McLaren	7	96
1992	Nigel Mansell	UK	Williams	9	108
1993	Alain Prost	France	Williams	7	99
1994	Michael Schumacher	Germany	Benetton	8	92
1995	Michael Schumacher	Germany	Benetton	9	102
1996	Damon Hill	UK	Williams	8	97
1997	Jacques Villeneuve	Canada	Williams	7	81
1998	Mika Häkkinen	Finland	McLaren	8	100
1999	Mika Häkkinen	Finland	McLaren	5	76
2000	Michael Schumacher	Germany	Ferrari	9	108
2001	Michael Schumacher	Germany	Ferrari	9	123
2002	Michael Schumacher	Germany	Ferrari	11	144
2003	Michael Schumacher	Germany	Ferrari	6	93
2004	Michael Schumacher	Germany	Ferrari	13	148
2005	Fernando Alonso	Spain	Renault	7	133
2006	Fernando Alonso	Spain	Renault	7	134
2007	Kimi Räikkönen	Finland	Ferrari	6	110
2008	Lewis Hamilton	UK	McLaren	5	98
2009	Jenson Button	UK	Brawn	6	95
2010	Sebastian Vettel	Germany	Red Bull	5	256
2011	Sebastian Vettel	Germany	Red Bull	11	392
2012	Sebastian Vettel	Germany	Red Bull	5	281
2013	Sebastian Vettel	Germany	Red Bull	13	397
2014	Lewis Hamilton	UK	Mercedes	11	384
2015	Lewis Hamilton	UK	Mercedes	10	381
2016	Nico Rosberg	Germany	Mercedes	9	385
2017	Lewis Hamilton	UK	Mercedes	9	363
2018	Lewis Hamilton	UK	Mercedes	11	408
2019	Lewis Hamilton	UK	Mercedes	11	413
2020	Lewis Hamilton	UK	Mercedes	11	347
2021	Max Verstappen	Netherlands	Red Bull	10	395.5
2022	Max Verstappen	Netherlands	Red Bull	15	454
2023	Max Verstappen	Netherlands	Red Bull	19	575
2024	Max Verstappen	Netherlands	Red Bull	9	437

DRIVER RECORDS

WORLD CHAMPIONSHIP MOST WINS
7 – Michael Schumacher **(1994, 1995, 2000, 2001, 2002, 2003, 2004)**

7 – Lewis Hamilton **(2008, 2014, 2015, 2017, 2018, 2019, 2020)**

MOST CONSECUTIVE WORLD CHAMPIONSHIP WINS
5 – Michael Schumacher **(2000, 2001, 2002, 2003, 2004)**

MOST CHAMPIONSHIP WINS WITH A SINGLE CONSTRUCTOR
6 – Lewis Hamilton **(Mercedes 2014, 2015, 2017, 2018, 2019, 2020)**

YOUNGEST WORLD CHAMPION
23 years and 134 days – Sebastian Vettel **(2010)**

OLDEST WORLD CHAMPION
46 years and 41 days – Juan Manuel Fangio **(1957)**

MOST GRAND PRIX WINS
105 – Lewis Hamilton **(2007-24)**

MOST GRAND PRIX WINS IN A SEASON
19 – Max Verstappen **(2023)**

MOST GRAND PRIX STARTS
401 – Fernando Alonso **(2001-24)**

MOST CONSECUTIVE GRAND PRIX STARTS
265 – Lewis Hamilton **(2007–20)**

MOST CONSECUTIVE GRAND PRIX WINS
10 – Max Verstappen **(2023)**

YOUNGEST GRAND PRIX WINNER
18 years and 228 days – Max Verstappen **(2016 Spanish Grand Prix)**

OLDEST GRAND PRIX WINNER
53 years and 22 days – Luigi Fagioli **(1951 French Grand Prix)**

MOST POLE POSITIONS
356 – Lewis Hamilton **(2007–24)**

MOST POLE POSITIONS IN A SEASON
15 – Sebastian Vettel **(2011)**

MOST CONSECUTIVE POLE POSITIONS
8 – Ayrton Senna **(1998–99)**

8 – Max Verstappen **(2023–24)**

MOST WINS FROM POLE POSITION
61 – Lewis Hamilton **(2007–21)**

MOST WINS FROM POLE POSITION IN A SEASON
12 – Max Verstappen **(2023)**

MOST FASTEST LAPS
77 – Michael Schumacher **(1992–2002)**

MOST FASTEST LAPS IN A SEASON
10 – Michael Schumacher **(2004)**

10 – Kimi Räikkönen **(2005, 2008)**

MOST PODIUM FINISHES
202 – Lewis Hamilton **(2007–24)**

MOST PODIUM FINISHES IN A SEASON
21 – Max Verstappen **(2023)**

MOST CONSECUTIVE PODIUM FINISHES
19 – Michael Schumacher **(2001–02)**

Max Verstappen holds a host of driver records

CONSTRUCTOR RECORDS

MOST CHAMPIONSHIP WINS

16 – Ferrari **(1961, 1964, 1975, 1976, 1977, 1979, 1982, 1983, 1999, 2000, 2001, 2002, 2003, 2004, 2007, 2008)**

MOST CONSECUTIVE CHAMPIONSHIP WINS

8 – Mercedes **(2014, 2015, 2016, 2017, 2018, 2019, 2020)**

MOST DRIVERS' TITLES

15 – Ferrari **(1952, 1953, 1956, 1958, 1961, 1964, 1975, 1977, 1979, 2000, 2001, 2002, 2003, 2004, 2007)**

MOST GRAND PRIX STARTS

1,098 – Ferrari **(1950–2024)**

MOST CONSECUTIVE GRAND PRIX STARTS

754 – Ferrari **(1982–2024)**

MOST GRAND PRIX WINS

248 – Ferrari **(1950–2024)**

MOST GRAND PRIX WINS IN A SEASON

21 – Red Bull **(2023)**

MOST CONSECUTIVE GRAND PRIX WINS

15 – Red Bull **(2022–23)**

MOST PODIUM FINISHES

632 – Ferrari **(1950–2024)**

MOST CONSECUTIVE PODIUM FINISHES

53 – Ferrari **(1999–2002)**

MOST PODIUM FINISHES IN A SEASON

33 – Mercedes **(2016)**

MOST POLE POSITIONS

253 – Ferrari **(1950–2024)**

MOST POLE POSITIONS IN A SEASON

20 – Mercedes **(2016)**

MOST CONSECUTIVE POLE POSITIONS

24 – Williams **(1992–93)**

MOST FASTEST LAPS

263 – Ferrari **(1950–2024)**

A celebration of Ferrari F1 cars over the years

Photography courtesy of Getty images

AFP / Stringer
Hulton Archive / Stringer
Heritage Images / Contributor
Dennis Oulds / Stringer
Popperfoto / Contributor
Gp Library / Contributor
Klemantaski Collection / Contributor
Rainer W. Schlegelmilch / Contributor
Central Press / Stringer
Rolls Press / Popperfoto / Contributor
Paul Popper / Popperfoto / Contributor
Mondadori Portfolio / Contributor
Grand Prix Photo / Contributor
Tony Feder / Stringer
Pascal Rondeau / Staff
Simon Bruty / Staff

Michael Kunkel / Staff
Anton Want / Staff
Tobias Heyer / Staff
Patrick Hertzog / Staff
Damien Meyer / Staff
Paul Gilham / Staff
Mark Thompson / Staff
Clive Mason / Staff
Prakash Singh / Staff
Dimitar Dilkoff / Staff
Keystone / Stringer
Bernard Cahier / Contributor
Express / Stringer
Paul-Henri Cahier / Contributor
Gabriel Duval / Staff
Bob Thomas / Contributor

Michael King / Staff
Bongarts / Staff
Mike Hewitt / Staff
Andrej Isakovic / Contributor
Guiseppe Cacace / Pool
Peter J Fox / Staff
Dan Istitene / Staff
Dominique Faget / AFP / Getty
Mark Sandten / Staff
Clive Rose / Staff
Hoch Zwei / Contributor
NurPhoto / Contributor
Ker Robertson / Staff
Lars Baron / Contributor
Peter Fox / Staff
Christian Bruna / Contributor

All other images Wiki Commons